ABANDONED SOUTHERN INDIANA

DEAD GRASS IN THE REARVIEW MIRROR

AMANDA BENNETT-COLE

FONTHILL

Fonthill Media Inc.
www.fonthillmedia.com
office@fonthillmedia.com

First published 2024

ISBN 978-1-62545-140-8

Typeset in Trade Gothic 10pt on 15pt
Printed and bound in England

CONTENTS

ABOUT THE AUTHOR

Amanda Bennett-Cole is based out of Lafayette, Indiana, where she pursues her interests of researching weird local history and recreational trespassing. At this point, she has distinct preferences for every GIS property search system in the Midwest region and will make it known. Besides research and exploring, she uses her free time to play video games, learn horrific vintage recipes, and spend quality time with her family and friends.

INTRODUCTION

Southern Indiana can be deceiving with all of its beautiful topography since the rest of the state is flat and mostly farmland. The Parke County Poor Asylum was one of the first places my best friend, Jenny, and I explored when we got back into the hobby. It took me close to five hours to track down the address for it through old medical journals and phone books from the early part of the 1900s. I still have it memorized. I've gotten incredibly good at finding locations based on vague directions; it's my superpower. Urban exploring is a secretive hobby for a good reason: if you find a pristine location that's completely untouched since it was abandoned, you definitely don't want others finding out, since one bad share can lead to edgy teenagers finding it, spray painting terrible graffiti everywhere, and breaking all the windows. Jenny, my exploring partner for the last twenty-plus years, and I like to revisit locations to get updated photos as they decay, and we are always disappointed if we walk in and the place has been trashed by some bored kids.

1

POOR FARMS/ASYLUMS/ INFIRMARIES: A BACKGROUND

A "poor farm" was a prevalent fixture in Indiana counties for the first twenty years following statehood. These establishments served as early social support components, offering food and shelter to persons living in poverty, whether young or elderly. According to Article IX, Section 4 of the Indiana Constitution from 1816, "Provide one or more farms to be an asylum for those persons, who by reason of age, infirmity, or other misfortunes may have a claim upon the aid and beneficence of society; on such principles, that such person find employment, and every reasonable comfort, and lose, by their usefulness, the degrading sense of destitution," the General Assembly was to establish poor farms. In general, local officials, particularly those at the township level, and the board of county commissioners, with the latter appointing personnel to the poor farms, were charged with carrying out state-enacted poverty relief regulations. Township trustees would interact with needy people personally and offer assistance. Although local officials continued to have direct responsibility over poverty relief, the statutory schemes that governed it underwent changes throughout time. Cory v. Carter, 48 Ind. 327, 339-40 (1874), a statute from 1830, required any free African American entering Indiana to post a $500 bond (equivalent to $14,000 presently), which was "conditioned that such person should not, at any time, become a charge to the county in which such bond was given, nor to any other county in the State." The law's main goal was to deter African Americans from moving to Indiana. (Fujawa)

Although many residents were unable to perform field work due to underlying disabilities, medical conditions, or advanced age, the poor farm's residents did work the land, raise crops, and maintain gardens in order to help provide food for the community and for sale. The yearly operating expenditures for all the farms in the state were $281,380, according to a state report on poor farms from 1895, while $24,187 was recovered from the sale of farm produce, which was typically the surplus not used by the occupants of the poor farm. It seems as though the term "inmates" was almost always used to describe those who lived at the poor farm, adding to the stigma of living there. To "break away from the stigma connected to the traditional name," legislation was introduced in 1943 to rename impoverished farms as "county residences." But it was frequently apparent, especially in local media, the baggage attached to the poor farm and the views toward those who lived there.

It has been reported that on the frontier, new settlers could suffer from a wide range of mishaps or injuries that could render them helpless. This made people vulnerable and destitute, especially in the early days of the frontier when there was little local familial support. People in these circumstances were referred to as "sick-poor." The existence of these "sick-poor" citizens, unable to sustain themselves because of disease, contributed to the variety of titles for many county poor farms, including the use of the terms "asylum" and "infirmary." People with physical or mental disabilities or chronic illnesses who were unable to support themselves frequently made the poor farm their default home. (Fujawa)

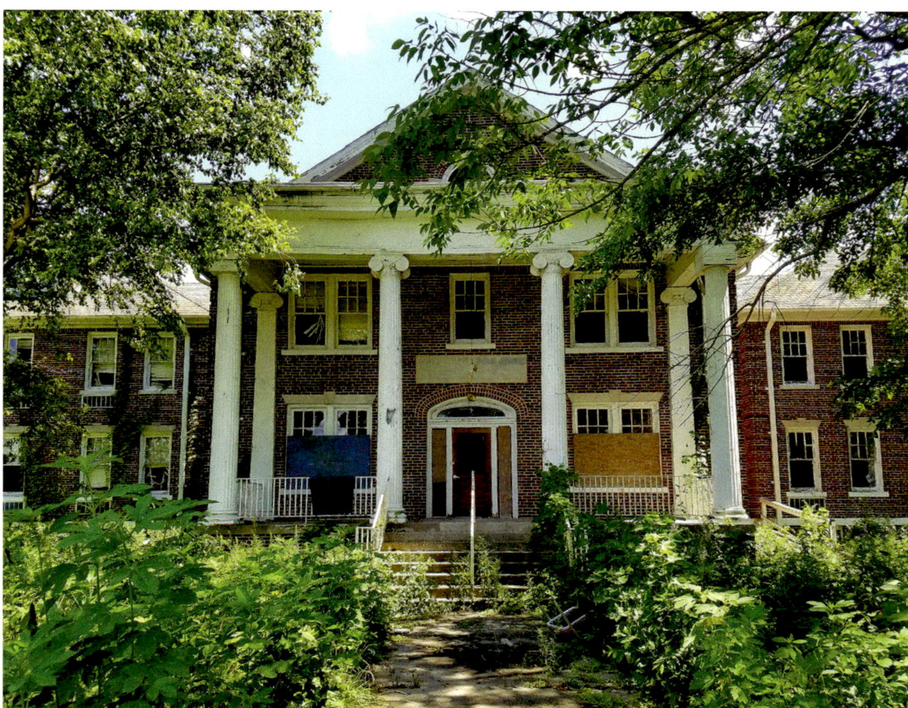

The front of the Parke County Poor Asylum.

2

PARKE COUNTY POOR ASYLUM

For the benefit of insane and sound paupers, the original structure was constructed in 1830; this building burnt down later that year. The Parke County Board of Commissioners received sealed bids on September 1, 1856, for a second poor asylum. The plans included a charge per week for both sound and insane impoverished persons covering all costs besides the material for the clothing and medical expenses incurred while caring for the paupers, as well as washing, nursing, boarding, mending, and manufacturing their own garments. The leasee was required to pay $120 a year in farm rent; half of the farm was to be kept in grass and the other half would be planted with different crops. Possession was granted on March 1, 1857, and Thomas F. Donaldson received a three-year contract from the commissioners to house the poor. He was to house and provide for the paupers for $60 per person per year, with the County covering all medical expenses. According to the contract, Mr. Donaldson was to receive the farm's earnings. According to Mr. Simpson, the editor of the local newspaper, it was thought to be a very low amount for housing the poor. "We have a tendency to believe that Mr. D won't profit greatly from his deal. The first day of March after that, he takes possession."

The county council allocated $26,000 in total for a new facility at the county poor farm in January 1907, including $10,000 more than the $15,000 previously appropriated and $1,000 for contingencies. This amount would have been enough to create a modern structure with adequate space to house everyone who was unlucky enough to be forced to rely on public charity.

On July 2, 1907, the commissioners awarded James T. Boswell of Bloomingdale a $30,000 contract to build the new county asylum building. By June 1, 1908, Mr. Boswell was to provide the keys to the board with everything prepared for occupancy. Wallace Brown of Rockville drew the blueprints and specifications.

In June of 1908, the County Board of Charities' annual examination of the poor asylum was conducted by members Rufus Dooley, president, C. B. Carver, secretary, Josiah Morris, Mrs. Francis R. Whipple, and Eli Carter. The new county building was carefully studied and universally praised. The board of directors found the ancient structure, which was still occupied, to be in as good of shape as could be expected given the circumstances, and Superintendent Tenbrook and his wife had taken excellent care of the unfortunate prisoners which received the board's unqualified approval. On April 10, 1930, a fire that was started by a hot wire in the southwest corner of the asylum's attic severely damaged the new structure. Around nine o'clock, an alert was received by the Rockville fire department. Fire Chief L. W. Brown discovered a collapsed roof when he arrived on the site. He quickly came to the conclusion that the structure couldn't be saved. The fire was contained to the main structure after the decision was made to save the walls for prospective future construction. During the fire fighting, the large Seagrave pumper had to be moved four times from one cistern to another due to the lack of water.

Homes that would welcome them opened immediately for the homeless infirmary residents. Some of the men preferred to stay within the other structures on the grounds of the county farm. All except one of the women were brought to the Vermillion County Hospital in Newport. (Historian)

Under the direction of Indiana-born architect, Carroll O. Beeson, a third structure was built in 1930. The Social Security Act of 1935 would pave the way for our current welfare system, making the 25,000-square-foot Neoclassical building one of the last few "poor homes" to be constructed. When a poor asylum was no longer necessary in the 1950s, the building—originally known as Parke County Nursing Home and then Parke County Residential Care Center—was turned into an assisted living facility. After permanently closing its doors in 2010, Mother Nature and vandals wreaked havoc on the institution, leaving it in ruins.

The building was acquired by a private party in March 2020, and it is currently undergoing the initial stages of restoration to become a private home.

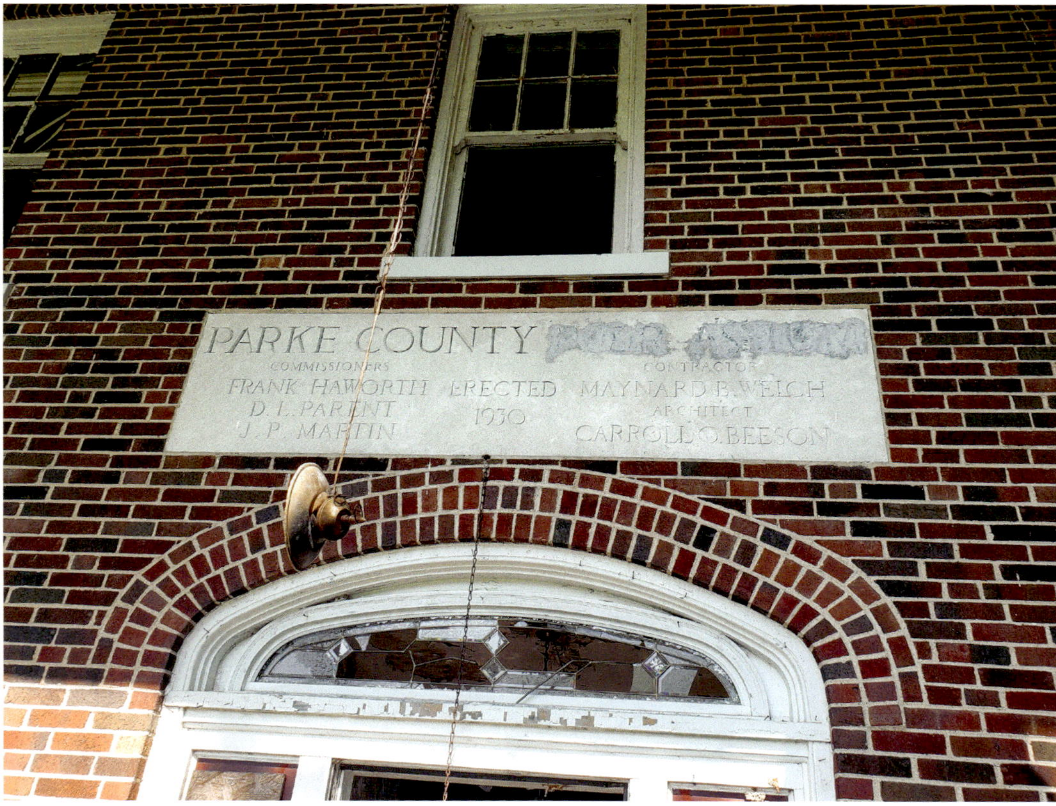

Above: A plaque commemorating when this particular building was built; at some point, they attempted to hide the "Poor Asylum" on the sign.

Right: The view from the inside to the front door.

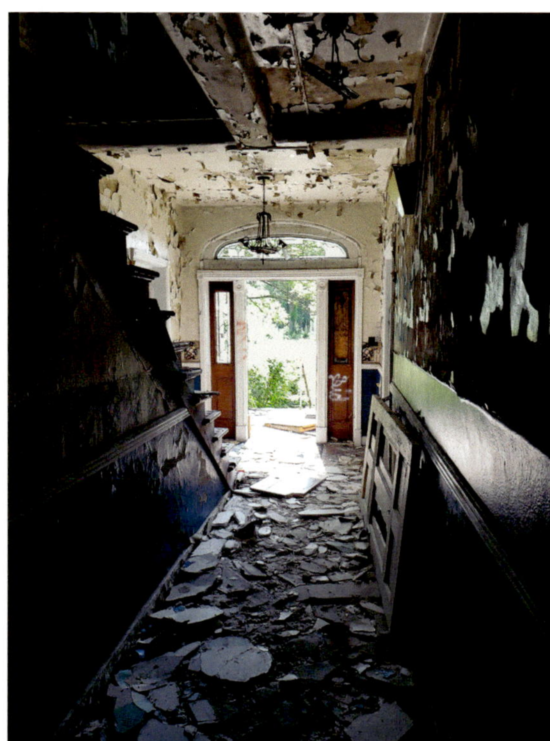

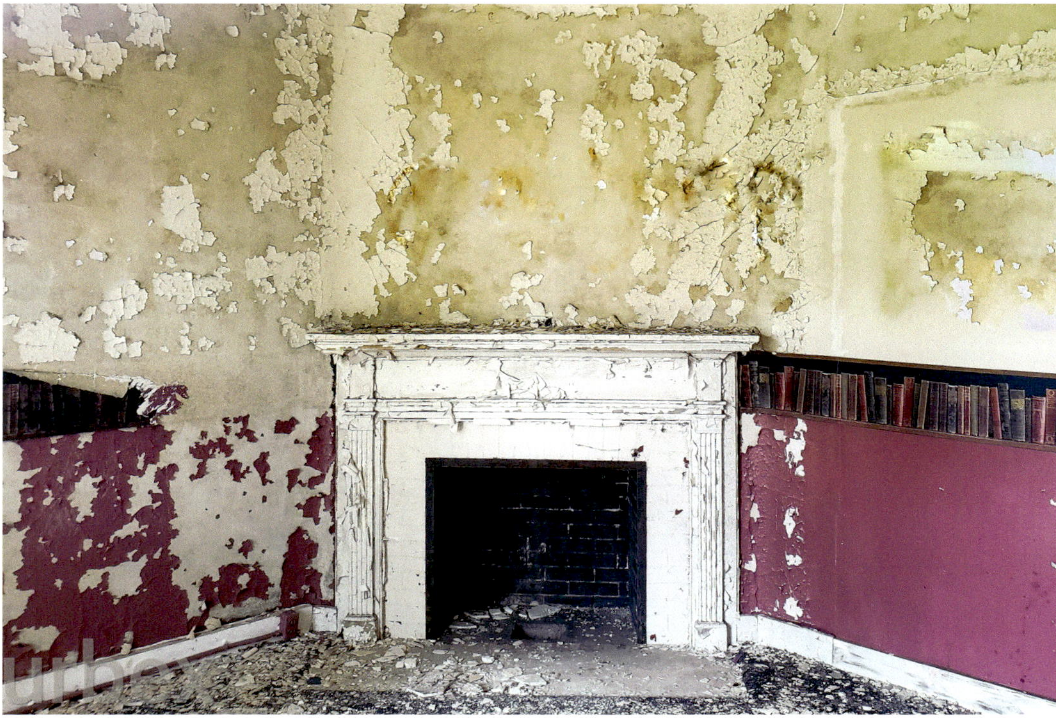

The fireplace in main living room, which is at the front of the building.

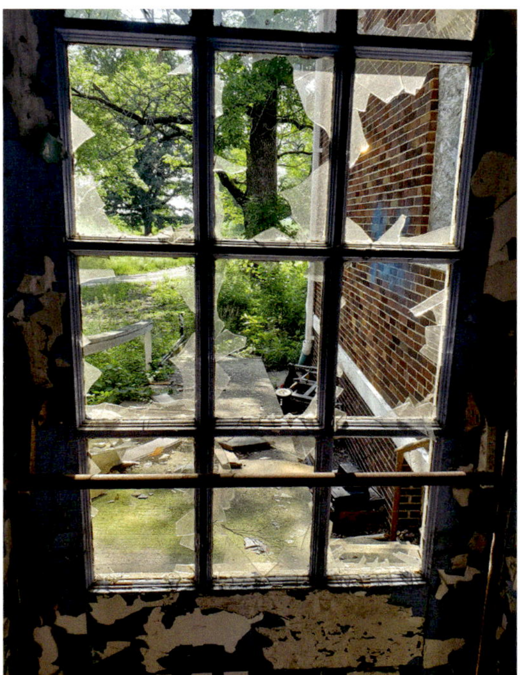

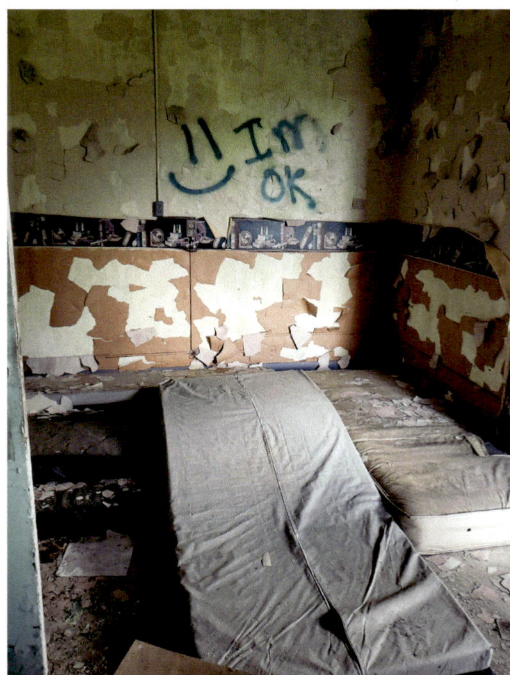

Above left: Almost all the glass was broken out of the windows and doors. This is one of the side doors.

Above right: A room full of mattresses, featuring some uplifting graffiti.

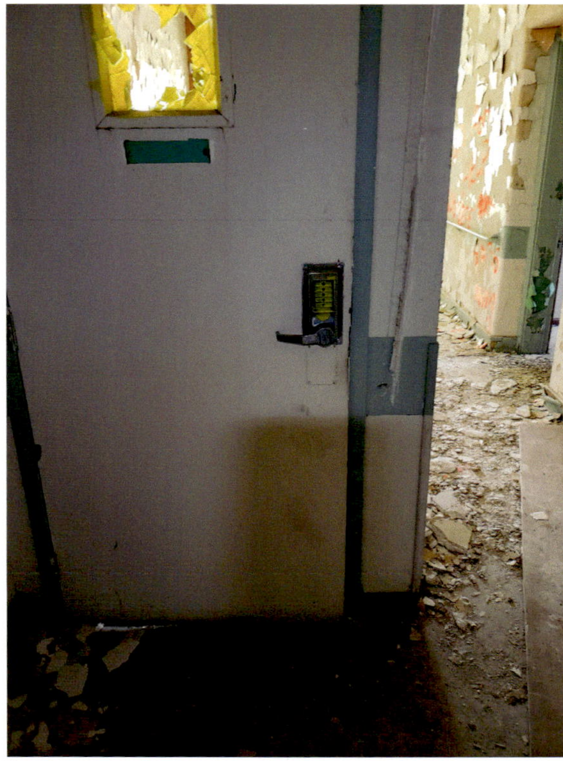

Secure stairway door on the second floor of the building.

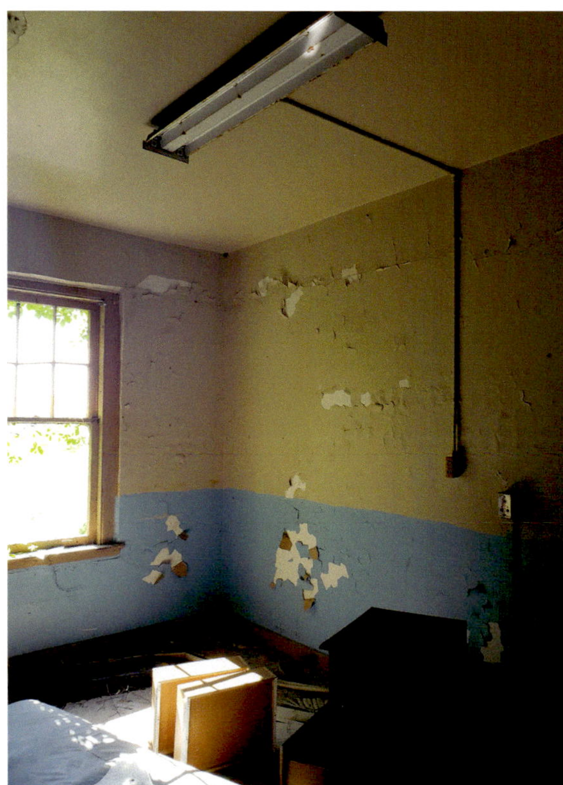

One of the resident rooms surprisingly had intact furniture left.

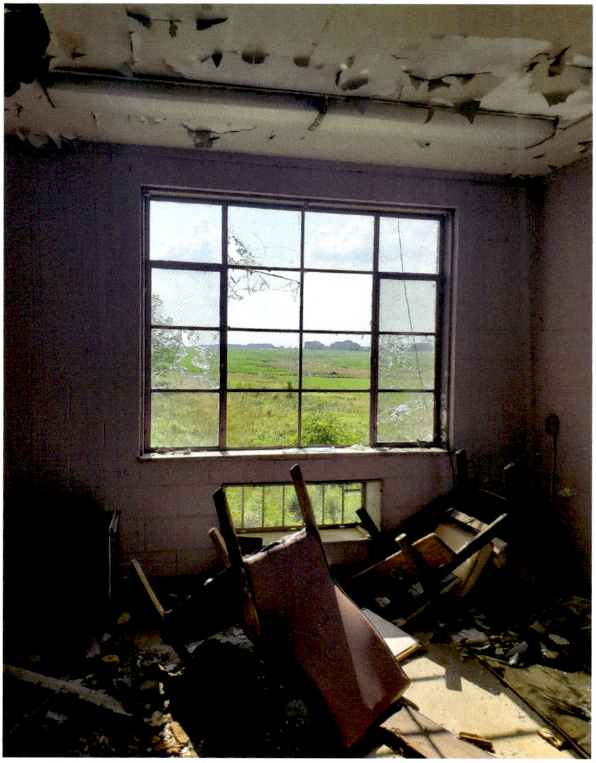

The top floor had two small sunrooms that housed chairs, couches, end tables, and some books.

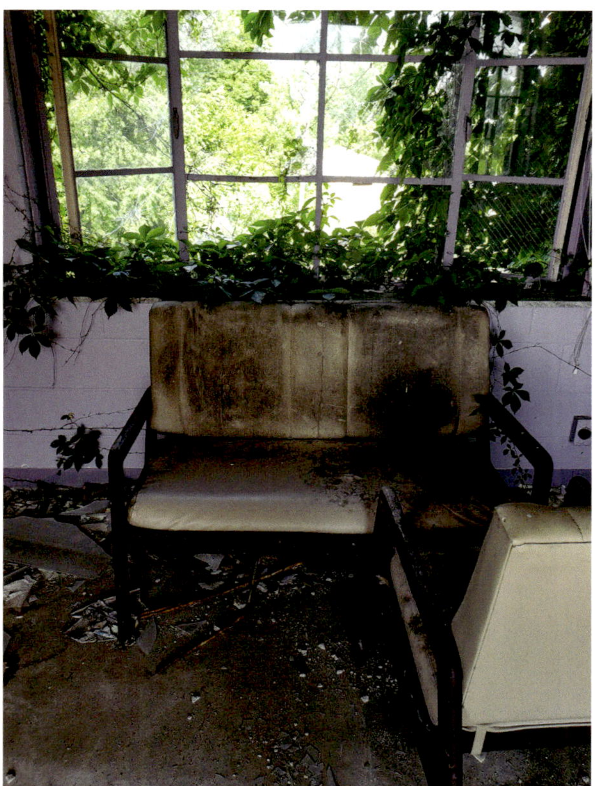

The second of the small sunrooms. This room had less furniture, but what was left wasn't thrown completely around.

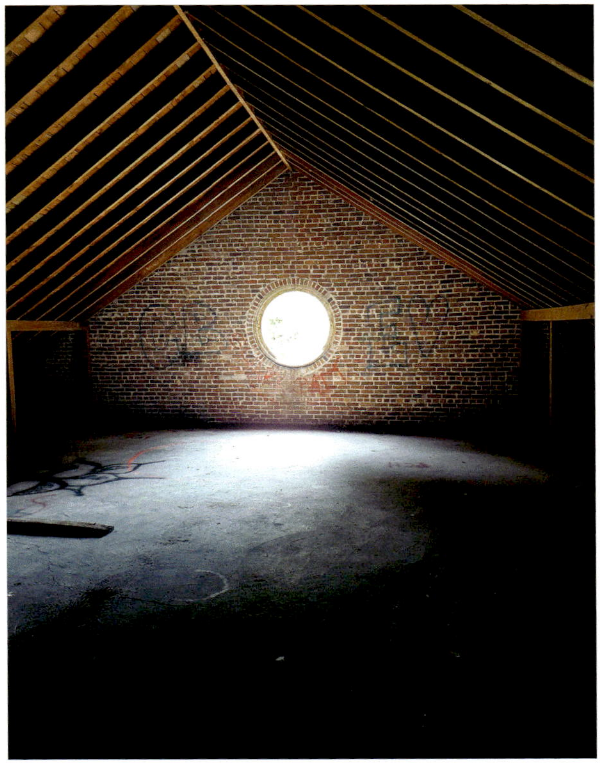

The attic was completely empty, which was honestly a welcome change compared to the rest of the building.

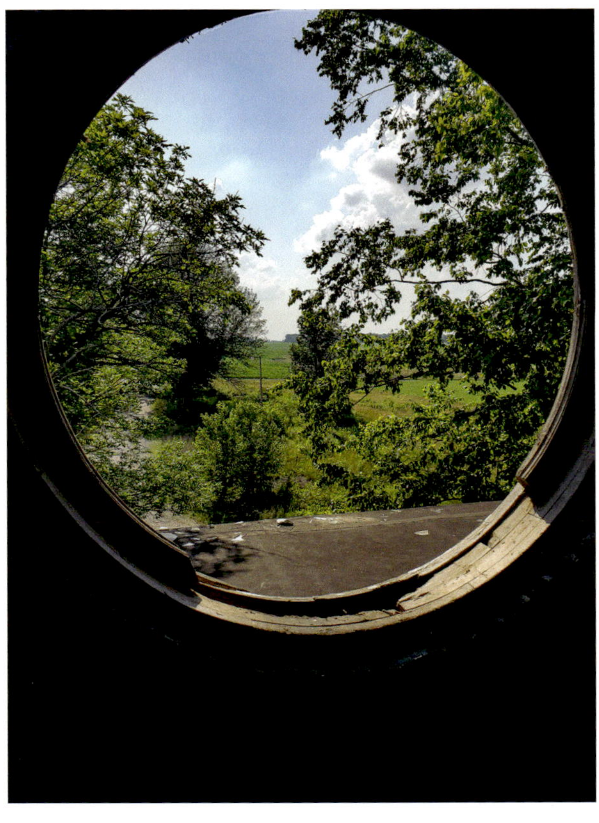

The view from the small window in the attic.

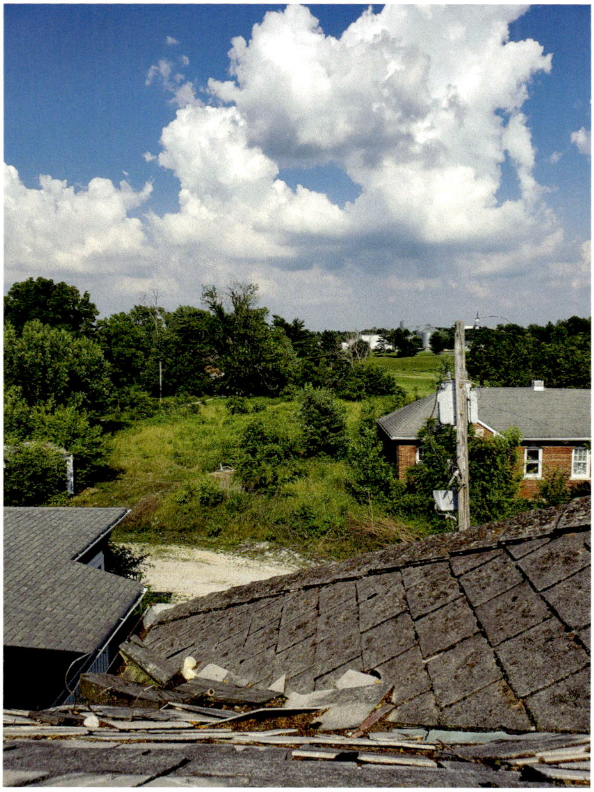

The view of the backside of the property from the roof; the next three photos were taken in the building on the left.

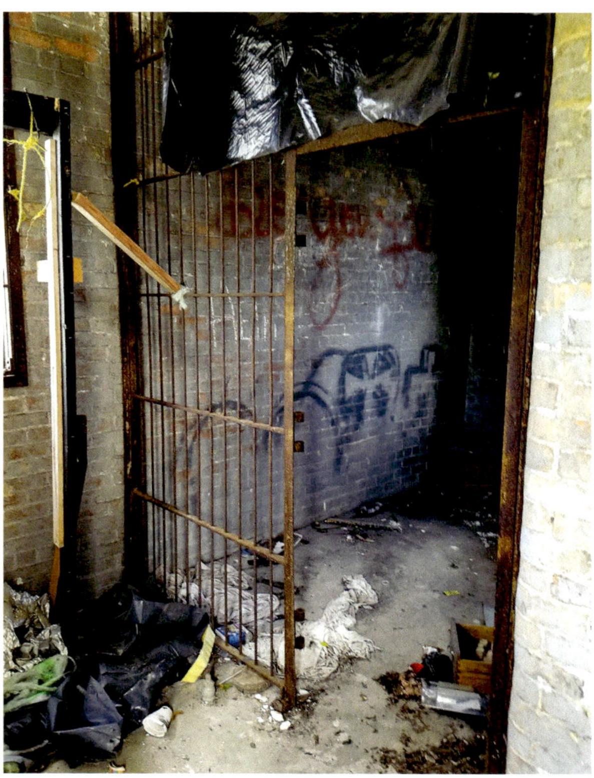

One of the two jail cells in the back building.

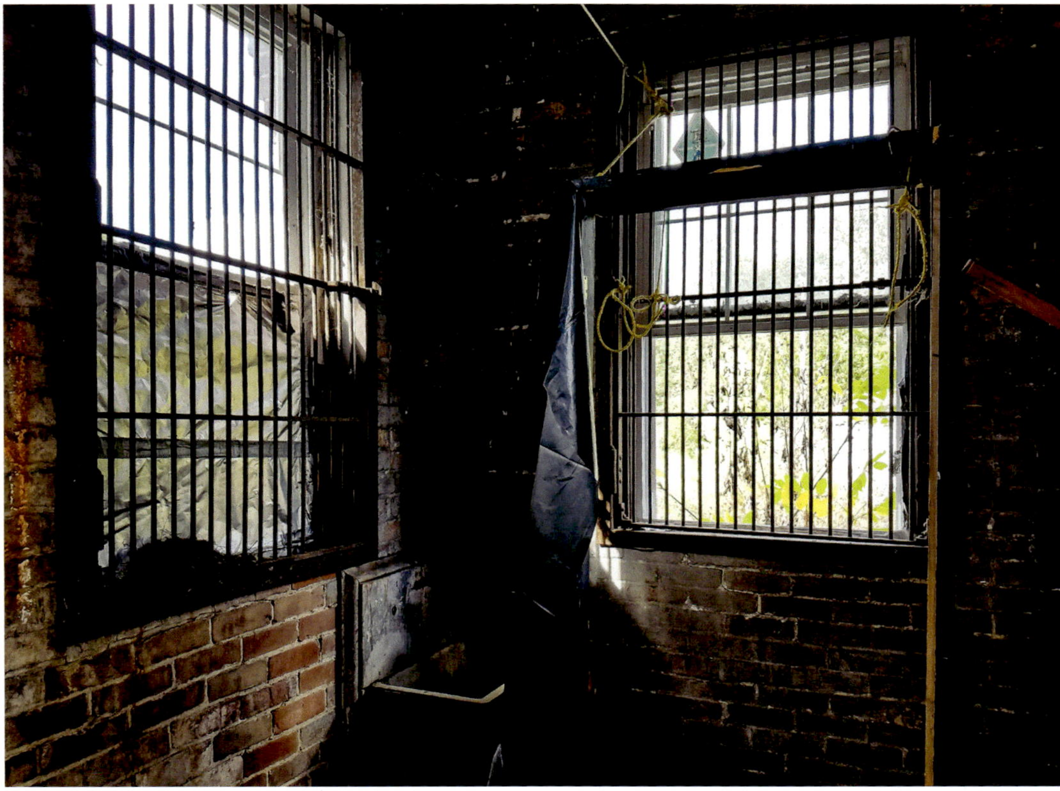

Above: Windows and a sink in the cell.

Right: The second cell had a lot more trash left behind in it, much of it from local teenagers.

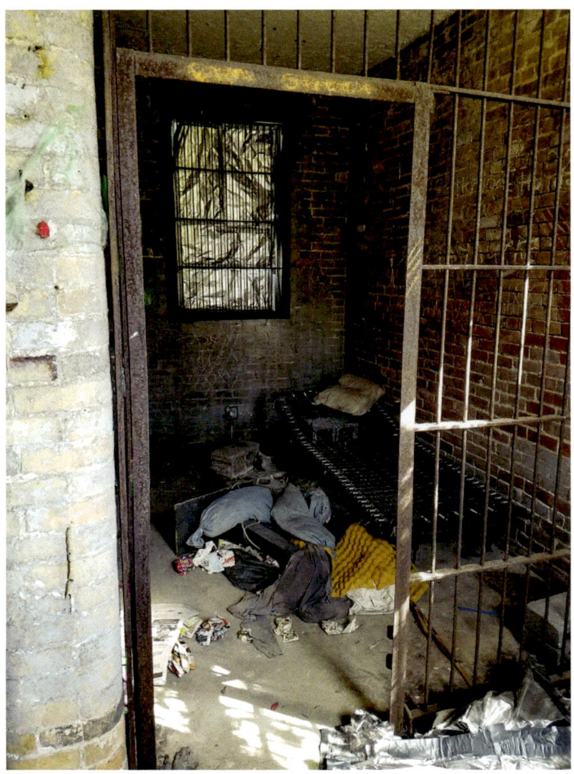

3

INDIANA STATE SANITARIUM

The Indiana State Sanatorium (1909–1968), also known as the Indiana Tuberculosis Hospital, and formerly the Lee Alan Bryant Healthcare Facility (1978–2012), was a state-run institution designated for the treatment and care of Tuberculosis patients located in Rockville, Indiana. The hospital was effective at treating the condition, and the overall fatality rate reduced. The low patient load led to the Sanatorium's closure in 1968. Private investors proposed turning the area into a nursing home in the middle of the 1970s, which led to the opening of the Lee Alan Bryant institution in 1978. This institution acquired an unfavorable reputation due to understaffing, which led to the state closing the facility in 2011. Before being bought in December 2020, the property languished abandoned for a decade.

A committee was established in 1905 by the state of Indiana to look into the necessity for a government-run institution. The state assembly had allocated $250,000 by 1907 for the acquisition of a location. To establish where the site should be located, a second committee was formed. The choice was made to buy 504 acres of land east of Rockville. The committee first requested funding to construct a hospital in 1909; this was shortly followed by the construction of an administration building, a power house, and two pavilions, one for men and the other for women, that flanked the administration building. For optimal access to fresh air, the main wards had porches that ran the length of the structure (a common practice against tuberculosis). The institution had a farm and laborers by 1911, and in 1918, a school was built, making it self-sufficient. In 1922, a superintendent's residence was erected, and two small bungalow-style residences for doctors were added after that. To move coal across Little Racoon Creek, the State Sanatorium covered bridge was built on site in 1913. (Reavis and Mahoney) Throughout its life, the grounds went through numerous alterations. The first significant alterations were made in the 1950s with the construction of a chapel in 1950 and "Adams Hall," a new five-story staff housing complex. This structure eventually underwent conversion to become a psychiatric hospital. Due to the development of a cure for tuberculosis by the end of the 1950s, the number of sufferers significantly decreased. As a result, the hospital was forced to close by the state in 1968 once it was unable to accept enough patients to stay open. Private investors and the state had intentions of converting the property into an assisted living residence by the 1970s. They suggested replacing the outdated tuberculosis unit between the Administration Building and Adams Hall with a new, contemporary facility. This was finished in 1978 and opened soon after. However, the hospital was plagued by a patient shortage. The state relocated patients from other state mental hospitals in an effort to take on more patients, which led to the mixing of patients who were considered to be "mentally ill" and those who required assisted living care. Because of poor treatment and inappropriate behavior, the hospital received a lot of criticism for mixing its patients, which led to several accidents and tragedies.

Multiple residents would wander away from the facility, only to be found deceased later. Myrtle Nordholt, seventy-one, strayed from the facility and passed away outside from exposure in January 2002. Derrick Rolewicz, thirty, a resident at the facility, hung himself less than a quarter mile away in April 2002. Following these fatalities, state inspectors demanded new locks for the residence's doors, raising concerns about limiting patients' rights. The majority of the home's residents are permitted to enter and exit the building as they want. Later in April 2002, a third resident wandered away, and the state Department of Health suggested putting the facility's license on probation. (*Tribune-Star*)

In March of 2005, the body of twenty-three-year-old resident, Severina Spivey, was found by a fisherman five miles away in Racoon Lake after being missing for over a month. Authorities concluded that she "sat down, laid down, went to sleep and froze." (Fashek) According to Spivey's mother, Jeana Ford, she had a protracted fight with mental illness. She was given schizophrenia and bipolar diagnoses in 1995 and 2004, respectively. Spivey received treatment at Merrillville's Southlake Center for Mental Health, but in 2004 the young woman started having more complicated relationships with the opposite sex, which led to Ford forcing Spivey to vacate her apartment, leaving Spivey without a place to live. Her temporary placement at Lee Alan Bryant came about as a result of doctors' efforts to find her a permanent assisted-living facility. Despite spending a lot of time with the man she had begun dating there, Spivey didn't seem to be doing well, according to Ford. Ford was informed by a Lee Alan Bryant administrator that Spivey had vanished on February 6 and that a search was ongoing. When Ford contacted the facility the next two days, she was informed that her daughter was still missing. Ford went to the Parke County Sheriff's Office on February 9 to report that her daughter was missing. As a result, the crew and volunteers from nearby fire departments undertook a thorough search of the nearby woods and vicinity. According to officials, nothing was discovered to aid the inquiry. No foul play was found after the autopsy. (Fashek)

In February of 2006, three days after the sixty-two-year-old Robert E. Didelot wandered away from his home at Lee Alan Bryant Health Care Facilities Inc., searchers came across his body in a creek, according to Parke County Sheriff Charles Bollinger. About 2-½ miles east of Rockville is the complex that comprises a nursing home and a residential institution. Near Sanatorium Bridge, "it seems [he] was trying to cross a log jam and slid out into the water," Bollinger added. According to the sheriff, the man ended up in water up to his neck. After several hours of searching, including a thorough search of the structure and the surrounding area, a staff member called the authorities, the sheriff said. (*Tribune-Star*) Didelot had lived at the facility for nineteen years, results from the autopsy found that he died of an epileptic seizure, which caused him to fall into the creek. (Hammer) George Porter, fifty-six, a resident of the Lee Alan Bryant Health Care Facility in Rockville in October 2006, was killed by a vehicle that struck him when he was walking barefoot on U.S. 36 early in the morning. According to authorities, the car's driver did not face any charges because he was unable to avoid hitting the man. Porter was standing in the middle of the road when he was struck, according to witnesses, said Parke County Sheriff Charles Bollinger, who also spoke with nursing home administrators. When the accident took place, "they told us they were searching for the person," Bollinger said. (*Tribune-Star*)

Deputies responded to a call from the Lee Alan Bryan healthcare center reporting a suspected suicide in August 2009; the shooting of an employee there was ultimately determined to be a drug-related "murder-suicide." Officers arrived on the scene and discovered Ryan Clark dead from a self-inflicted head wound. Kenneth Godfrey, a colleague of Clark's, had been reported missing. He had one gunshot wound to the chest when he was found dead on the floor of a neighboring maintenance building. Investigators think Clark entered the maintenance building, killed Godfrey, and then returned to the boiler room to commit suicide. According to a toxicology study, Clark had marijuana and benzodiazepines in his bloodstream. Investigators believe Clark believed he should have been responsible for rebuilding a water pump, and according to Parke County Sheriff Mike Eslinger, Godfrey had been given the go-ahead by superiors. Godfrey had been given the task of rebuilding a water pump, which Clark, according to investigators, believed should have been his duty. Eslinger noted that the situation had "festered" and said, "So it just went downhill from there." According to reports, Clark called his place of employment that day at about 2:00 p.m. to say he would be absent. However, police suspect Clark arrived later and shot Godfrey before killing himself. They had been coworkers for almost nine years. There was no proof that the disagreement went beyond the specific workplace problem. (Boyce)

The fatalities surrounding the location weren't the only issues leading to its closure. On May 17 and June 8 in 2004, two Lee Alan Bryant Health Care Facility patients filed separate complaints with the state. Director of public affairs for the health department, Margaret Joseph, stated that any facility from which a grievance is received must undergo an obligatory survey. On June 10–11, June 14, June 22, and June 25, the state dispatched three registered nurses to survey the facility at 3838 East Old U.S. 36 Road. Since the complaints were rated as having the second-highest severity, according to Joseph, they were resolved within thirty days. She added that the most serious complaints would demand immediate attention. Interviews were conducted with thirteen individuals, including the two who had initially complained, and thirteen certified nurse assistants. According to a press statement, the inquiry showed the facility "failed to guarantee that patients had been free from mental, verbal, and sexual abuse." The survey report claims that one CNA saw two employees in the dining room encourage a resident to "lift her shirt, expose her breasts, [and] ask male residents present in the dining room to engage in sexual conduct." The resident's records reflect a history of dementia and schizophrenia. According to the article, the CNA said that her coworkers made fun of the incident. The same CNAs, according to another CNA, were "talking about sex and lovers" and encouraging the patient to use explicit language. According to the report, the CNA saw the woman lift her top and reveal her breast. As reported by a different CNA who was interviewed for the survey, the same CNAs instructed another individual who had a history of "self-abusive behavior as evidenced by striking himself in the head and or genitals" to strike himself in the genitalia. According to the complaint, the CNAs laughed at the man for punching himself.

Further in the complaint it was alleged that the administrator and director of nursing thought these and previous occurrences like them were "horseplay." The two CNAs were terminated from their positions at the institution on June 25 and put on probation until the inquiry was finished, according to the report. The institution "neglected to assure suitable temperature(s) in two of four resident halls, one of two dining areas, and six of fifty resident rooms," according to the survey. The survey report states that the facility's policy is to maintain temperatures between 71 and 81 degrees. The report reveals that during the inspection on June 10–11, surveyors asked maintenance staff to use infrared thermometers to measure temperatures, which ranged from 81.3 to 94 degrees. According to Joseph, the institution was requested to submit a plan of rectification for the two infractions by July 14; the plan was received on July 19. The problems had been fixed, according to a follow-up survey conducted on September 2. (Mullins)

2004 also saw a former member of staff be convicted of battery. Virginia Mitchell, a former employee of Lee Alan Bryant, was charged with assault in April 2004 for allegedly mistreating people entrusted to her care. Mitchell acknowledged in her plea deal that she had touched a patient inappropriately. According to Parke County Prosecutor Steve Cvengros, "She stated she had put the hand of one [male] patient on the breast of [a female] patient." Mitchell was sentenced to 180 days in prison, all of which were suspended save for the time already served, a year of unofficial probation, and no contact with the victims after entering a guilty plea to battery, a class-B misdemeanor. (*Tribune-Star*)

The Lee Alan Bryant Health Care facility's license was put on second-time probation in 2007 after the Indiana State Department of Health (ISDH) filed an action in this regard. According to an ISDH news release, it was found that the institution was operating against state regulations governing long-term care facilities. After an examination into a complaint and the end of an ISDH licensure survey for annual recertification, it was determined that the health or safety of some residents was in immediate danger. The facility received a citation from the ISDH for failing to: ensure nursing staff responded quickly to a resident experiencing respiratory distress; consider a suctioning procedure to solve the issue; stop continuous gastrostomy feeding of a resident with respiratory distress; and have suctioning equipment in the room for use by residents in respiratory distress. (Followell)

The 2009 Annual Report for the Protection and Advocacy for Individuals with Mental Illness (PAIMI) reported that an anonymous caller to Indiana Protection and Advocacy Services informed them that a resident at the Lee Alan Bryant (LAB) Room and Board Assistance facility had died as a result of maltreatment. The decedent had allegedly suffered from severe diarrhea and weight loss in the week before his death, and the caller claimed no medical assistance or intervention was given by employees. Records analysis revealed that the deceased was a forty-five-year-old male with an extensive medical history, including schizophrenia and diabetes diagnoses. After reviewing agency regulations and interviewing workers, PAIMI staff discovered that LAB had neglected to inform any of the pertinent agencies of the client's passing. The personnel of the facility were compelled by the P&A's findings to submit the required notifications to Adult Protective Services (APS) and ISDH. The inadequacy of the facility's staff to adhere to its own internal policy in relation to examining and analyzing

"Unusual Occurrences" was also brought up to the facility's administration by APS. Consequently, PAIMI staff monitored the investigative actions of the institution, ISDH, and the local Coroner. The three parties came to the conclusion that, in accordance with the provider's operating norms, neither abuse nor negligence contributed to the client's death; rather, it was caused by desquamative pneumonitis. All personnel were retrained on the facility's Policies of Incident Reporting as a result of the P&A's determination that staff had failed to report incidents in a timely manner. (Protection and Advocacy for Individuals with Mental Illness)

The facility continued operations until 2011 when they were closed due to lack of funding. Residents of the Lee Alan Bryant Health Care Facility in Rockville were advised they were required to transfer after the Indiana Family and Social Services Administration's contract with the program's Residential Care Assistance Program was not renewed. RCAP offers residential financial support to qualified individuals who are blind, crippled, or at least sixty-five years old and residing in licensed care facilities. The facility's state licensure survey, which was conducted on November 19, 2010, uncovered six problems listed by the state Health Department. These shortcomings concerned the cleanliness of the facility, the equipment and areas used for food service, the amount of hot water available for bathing and handwashing, the assessment of resident needs, the documentation of medication and treatment administration, and the quality of the facility's food and nutritional services. (Trigg)

A January 2019 newsletter for Parke County details how since the State of Indiana stopped supporting the operation, the facility has been unoccupied. Asbestos was discovered on the seven-acre parcel through environmental assessments, the firm that held the deed to the property was dissolved, and property taxes have not been paid by the lien holder since 2010. Over the preceding three years, the state and Environmental Protection Agency have requested assistance on numerous occasions in order to resolve this situation. The State of Indiana announced in the fall of 2018 that they would pay for the groundwater inspection and asbestos cleanup provided the county agreed to seek ownership through the delinquent property tax process. The commissioners verbally agreed to do this in exchange for the Indiana Department of Environmental Management (IDEM) putting their plans into writing and agreeing not to hold the County liable for any potential later-discovered toxins. (Partnership Parke County)

Due to the state of the entire world in 2020, these ideas were pushed to the back burner; however, the facility was purchased by Gregg Larson late in 2020. Larson has opened the facility up for numerous tours and has plans for further revitalizing the site.

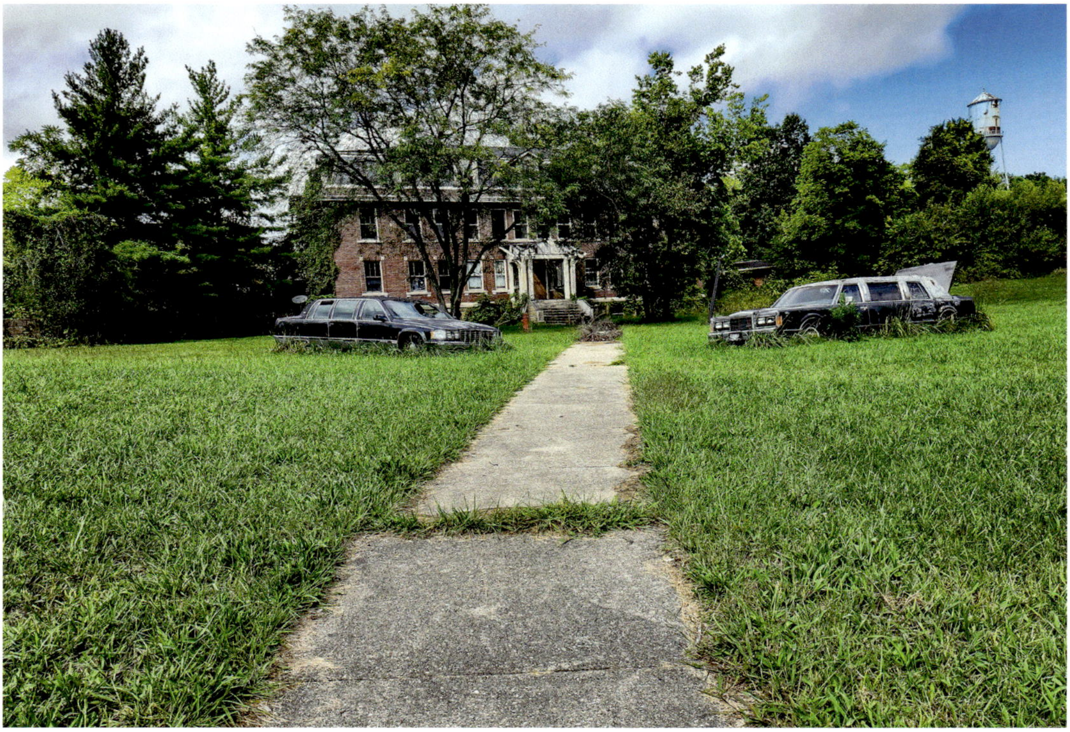

Walking towards the original building that housed tuberculosis patients from the main road.

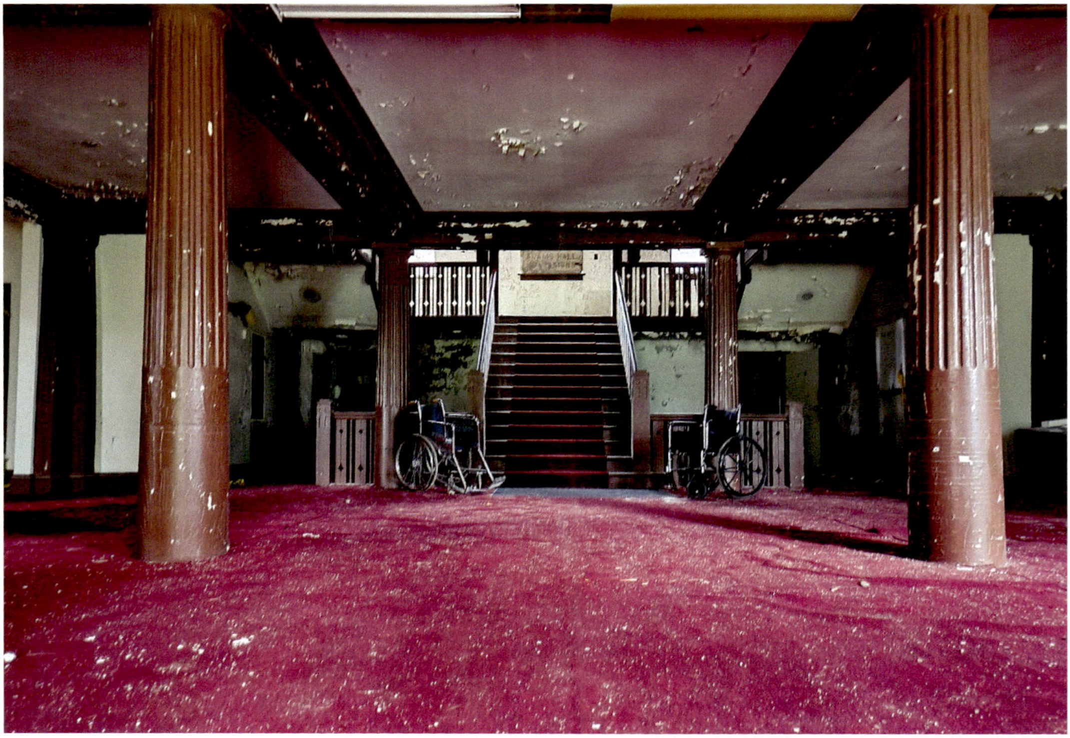

The foyer of the main building. The carpet has kept its color surprisingly well.

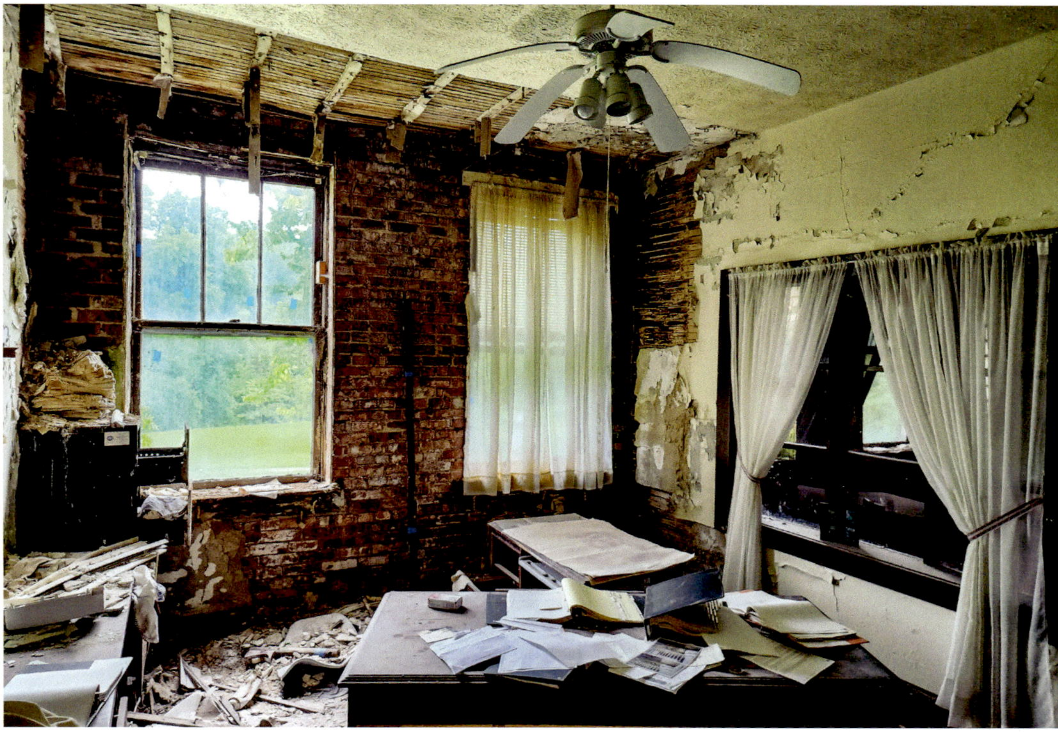

This is the administrative office where people would check in. There were still family photos left behind.

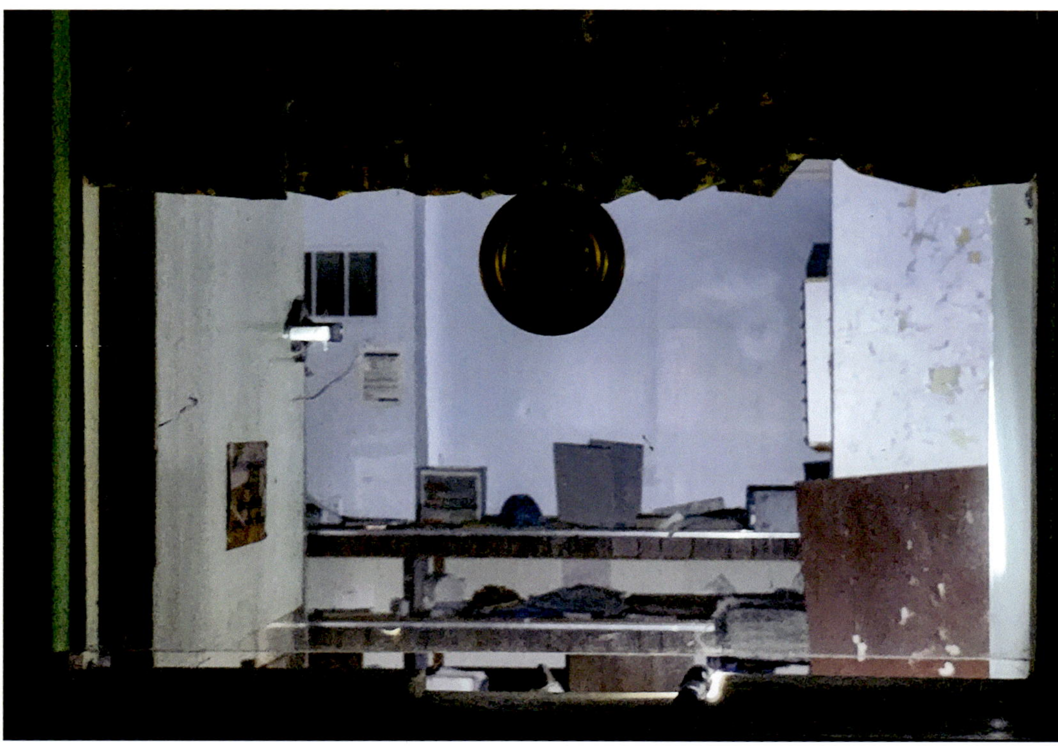

This is the office where patients would be able to access their money (but only on certain days and certain times).

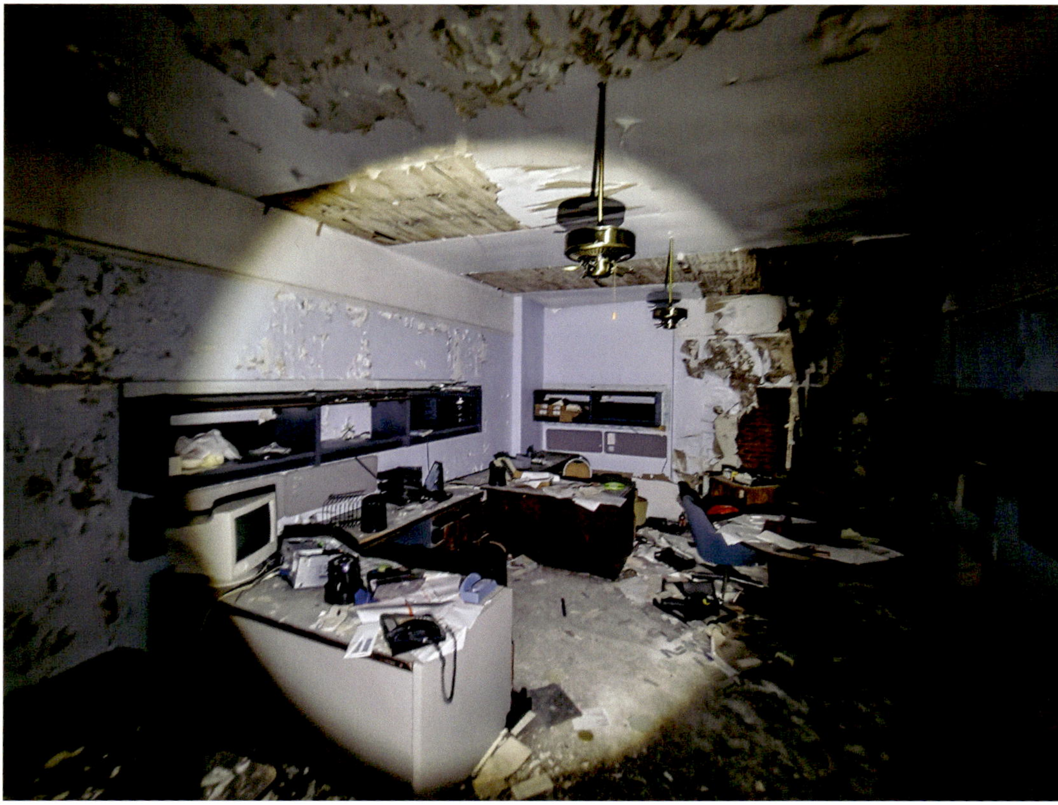

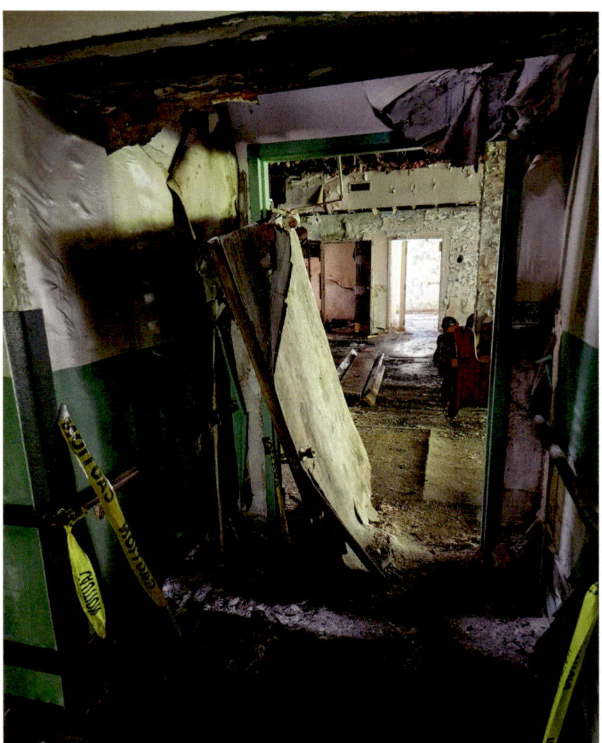

Above: Inside the office you can see where the paint has started peeling due to neglect. On the desks were personal calendars, phone bills and more personal objects.

Left: Entrance to the great room. This area had extensive water damage, which is why the door became warped and floppy.

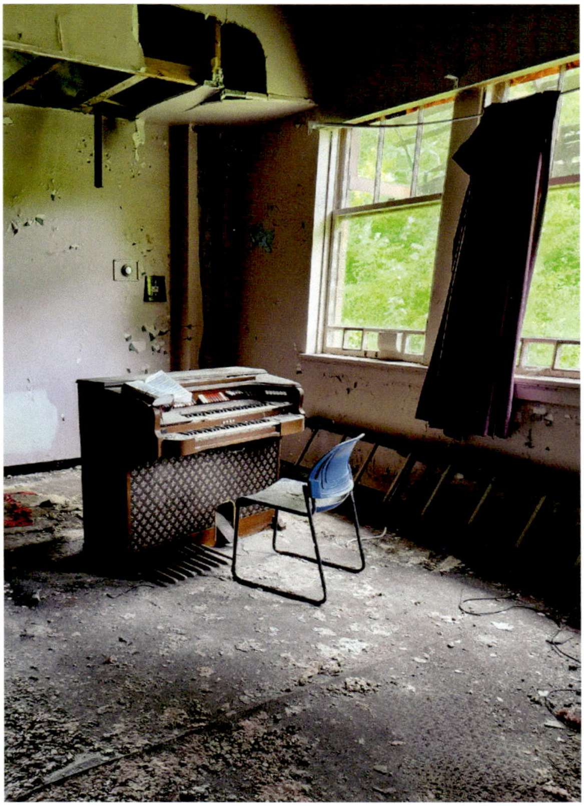

Right: The piano that was left behind in the great room. This would be where residents participated in recreational activities.

Below: One of two large paintings of Jesus that hung on the walls.

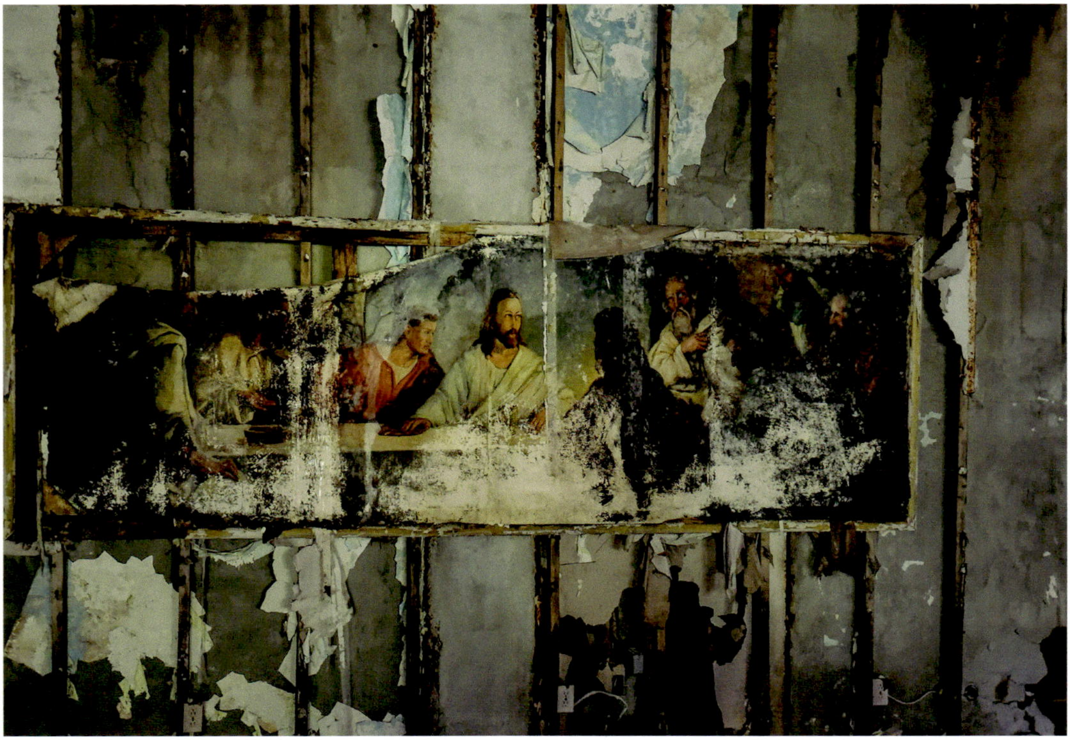

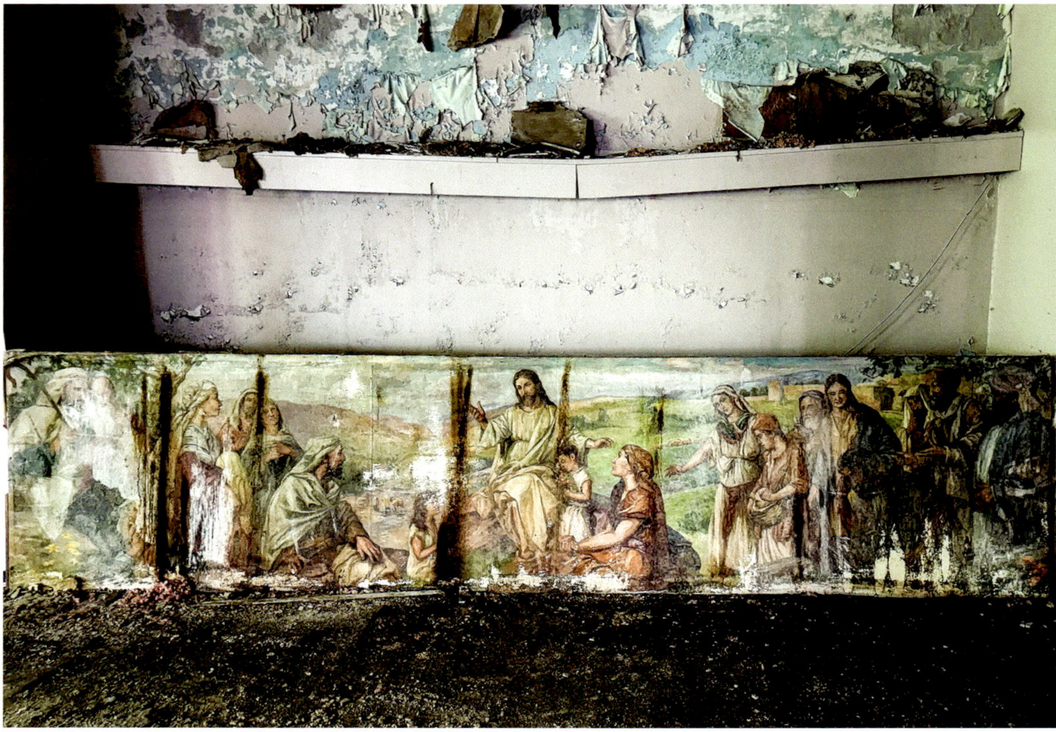

The second painting lies on the floor. Both have significant water and mold damage.

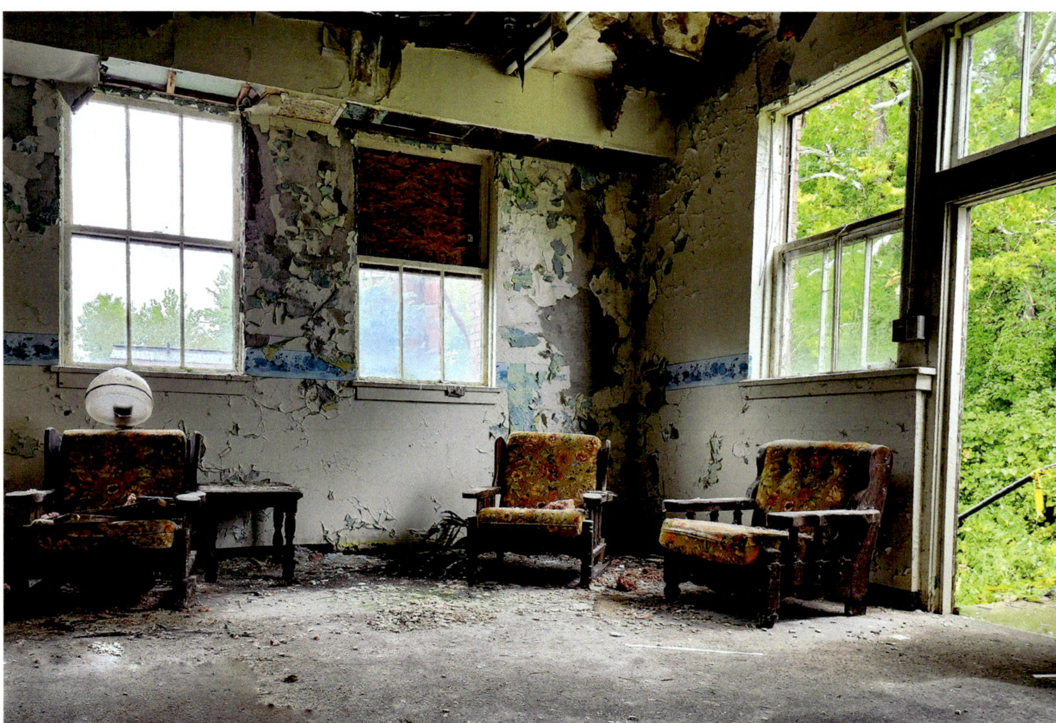

The beauty parlor which is accessed through the great room.

Right: The color scheme in this room was all around fantastic, but these dryers were my favorite.

Below: Full room shot of the beauty parlor. Almost all the windows had been broken out and the door no longer exists.

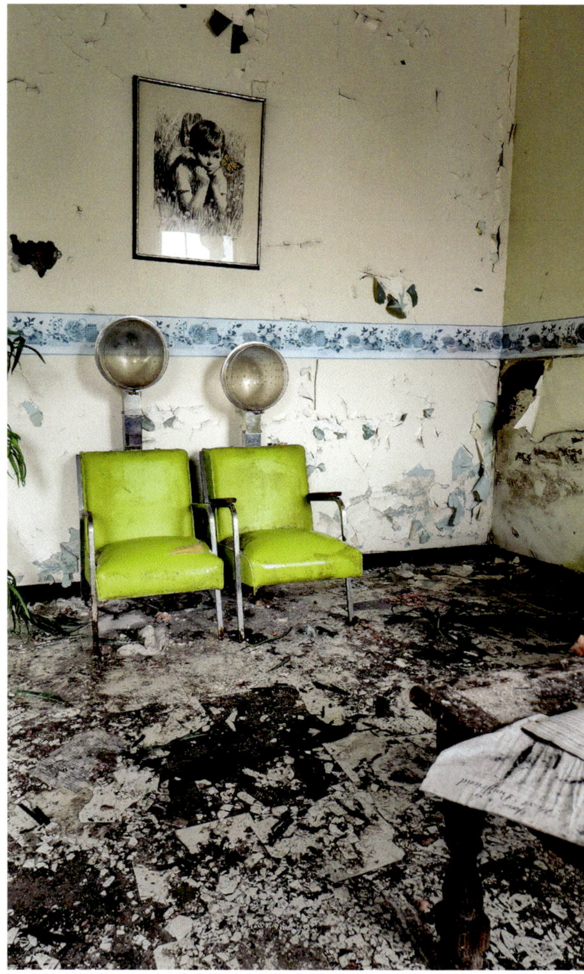

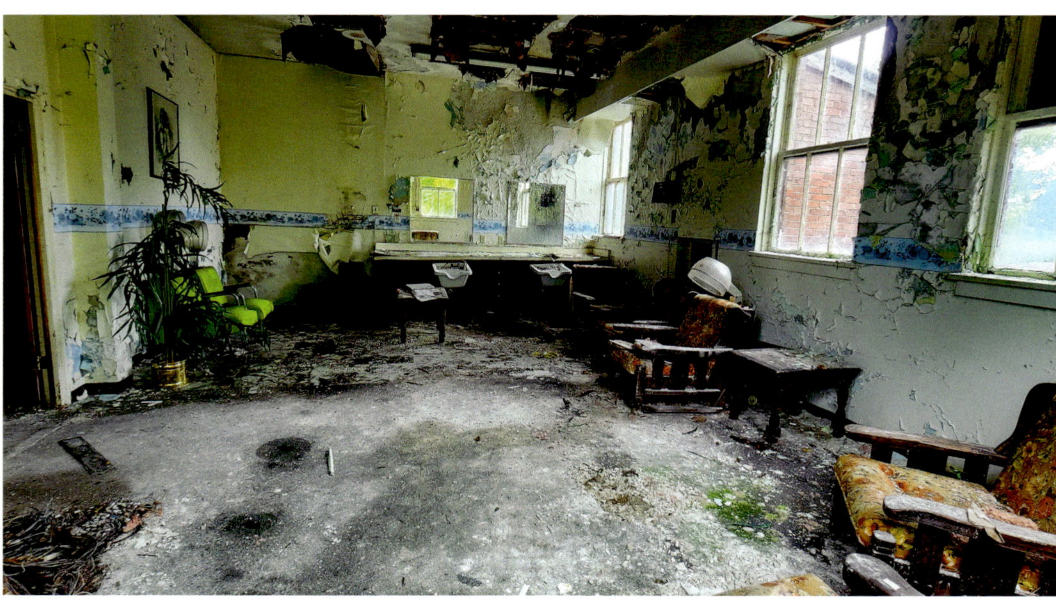

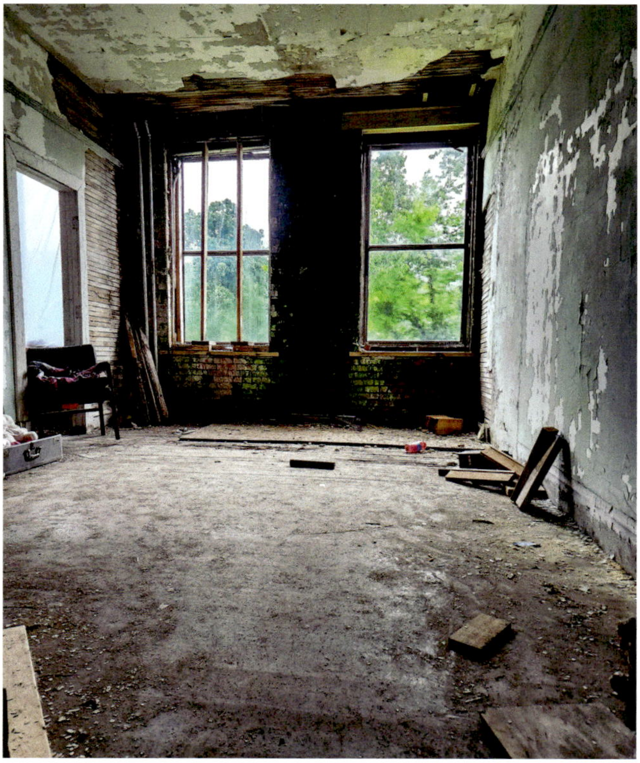

At one point, a former owner was offering bits and pieces of the institution as architectural salvage; this room was almost completely stripped.

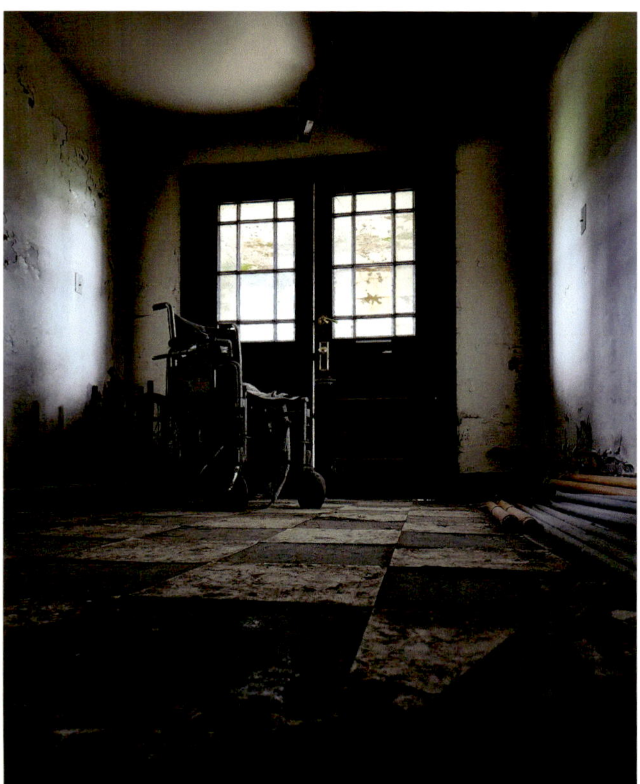

A wheelchair in front of one of the first-floor side doors; it was completely rusted shut.

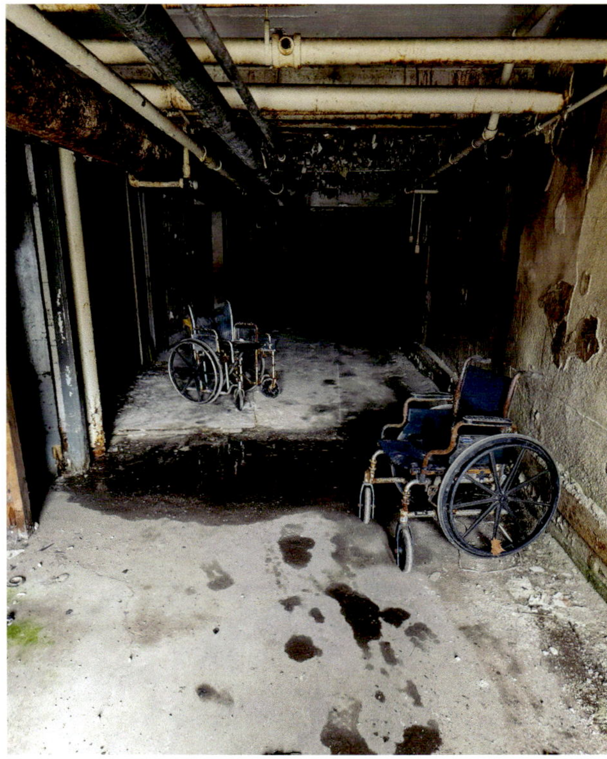

As is the case with most large multi-building institutions, there are tunnels running underneath that connect all the buildings. This is the entrance under the original building.

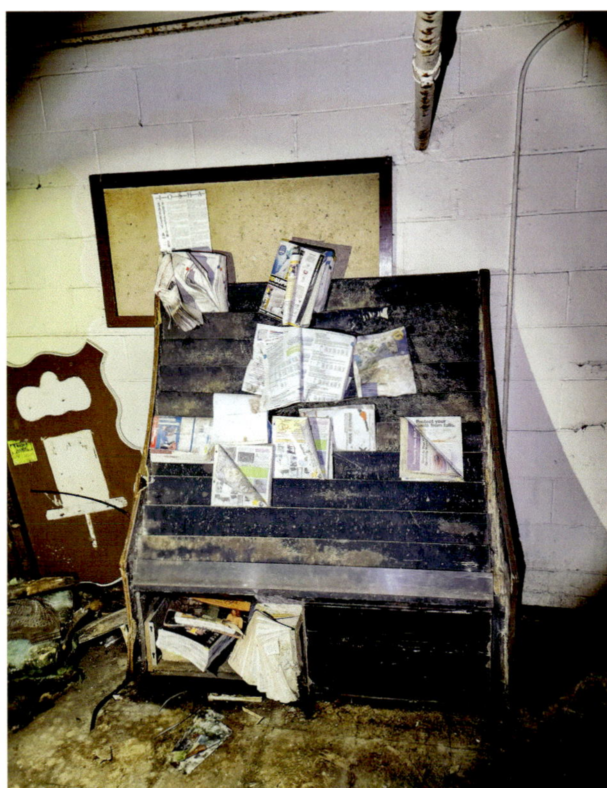

A magazine/brochure rack left in the basement along with a bulletin board featuring an OSHA letter.

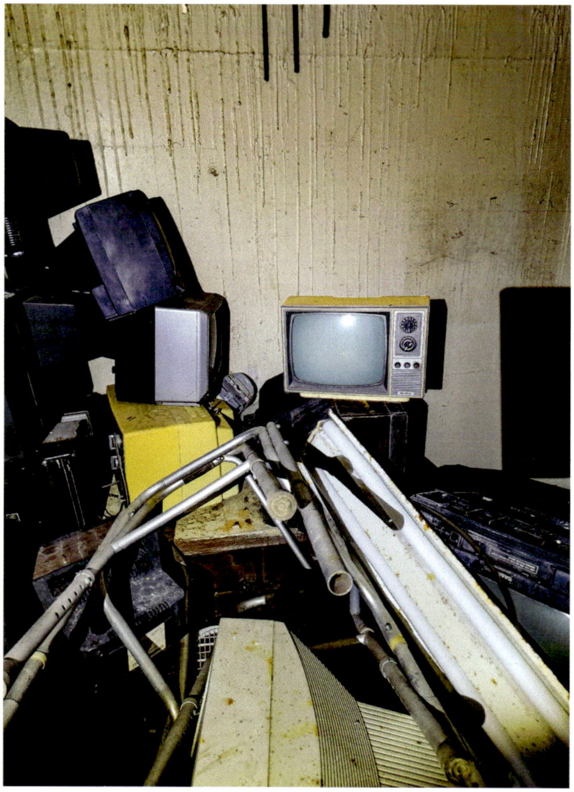

One of my favorite things to find are old TVs, and this area had a tower of them.

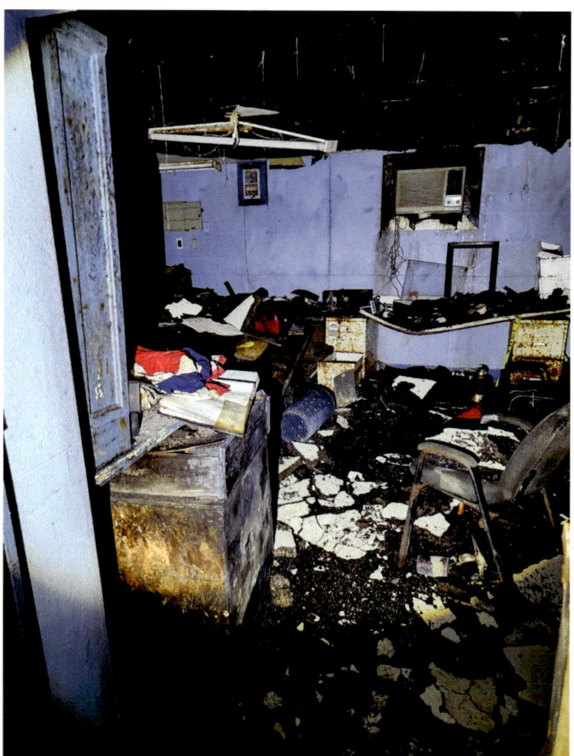

In the maintenance office, the ceiling tiles had entirely collapsed, forming a moldy sludge that we decided not to walk through.

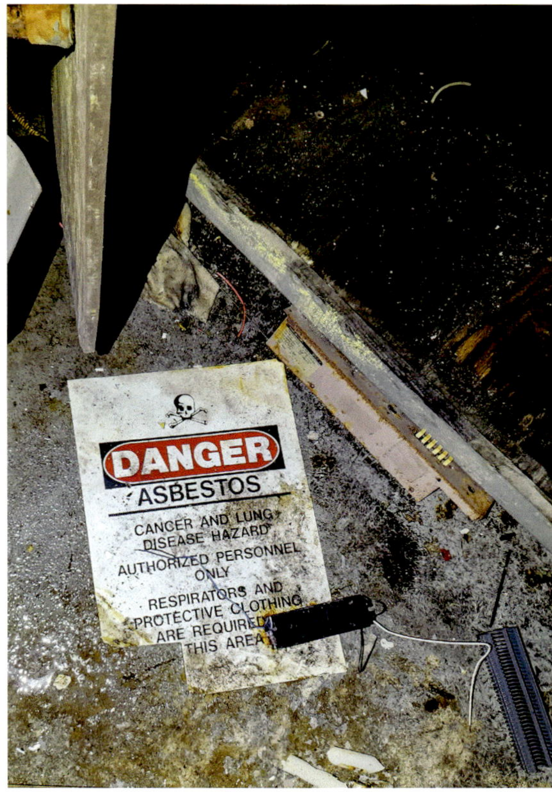

Warning sign for asbestos left in the basement. This and mold are why we always wear masks in abandoned buildings.

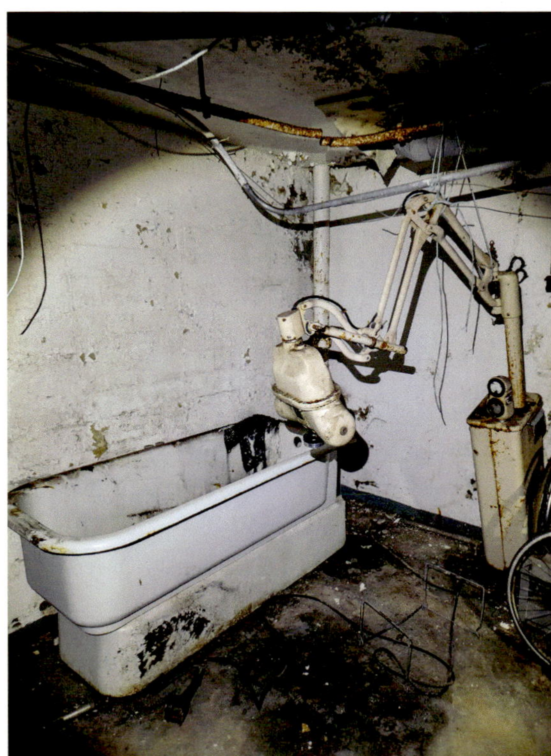

Bathtub and mystery medical equipment left in the corner of the basement.

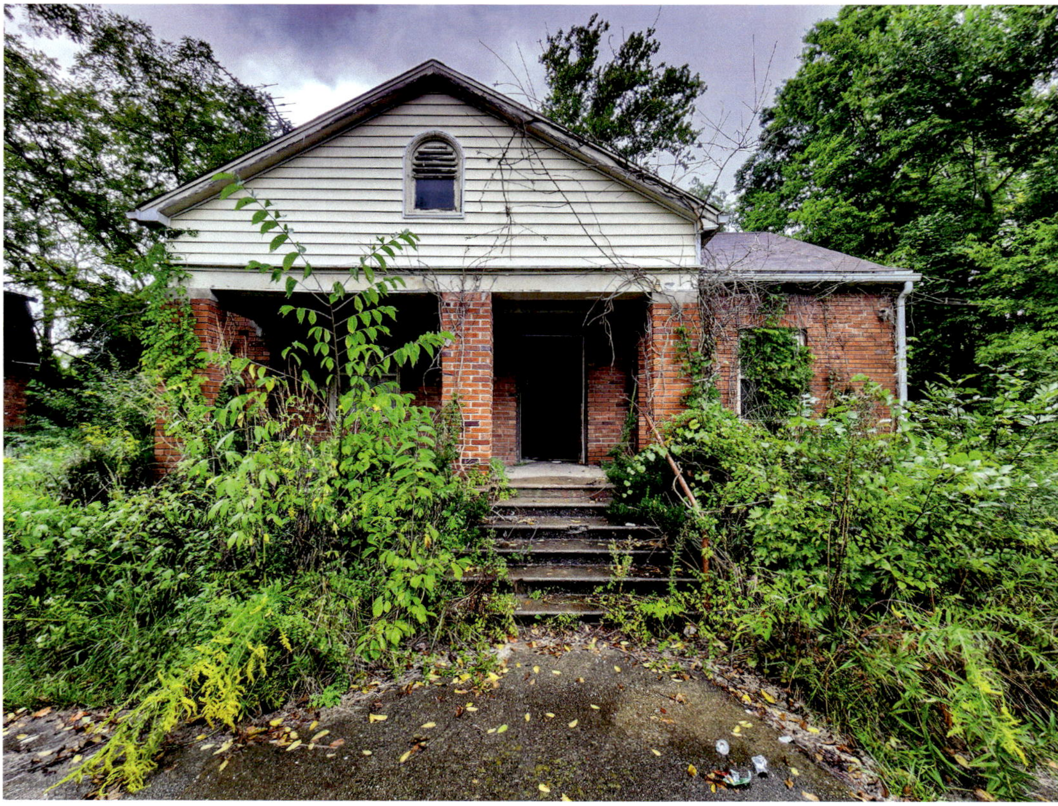

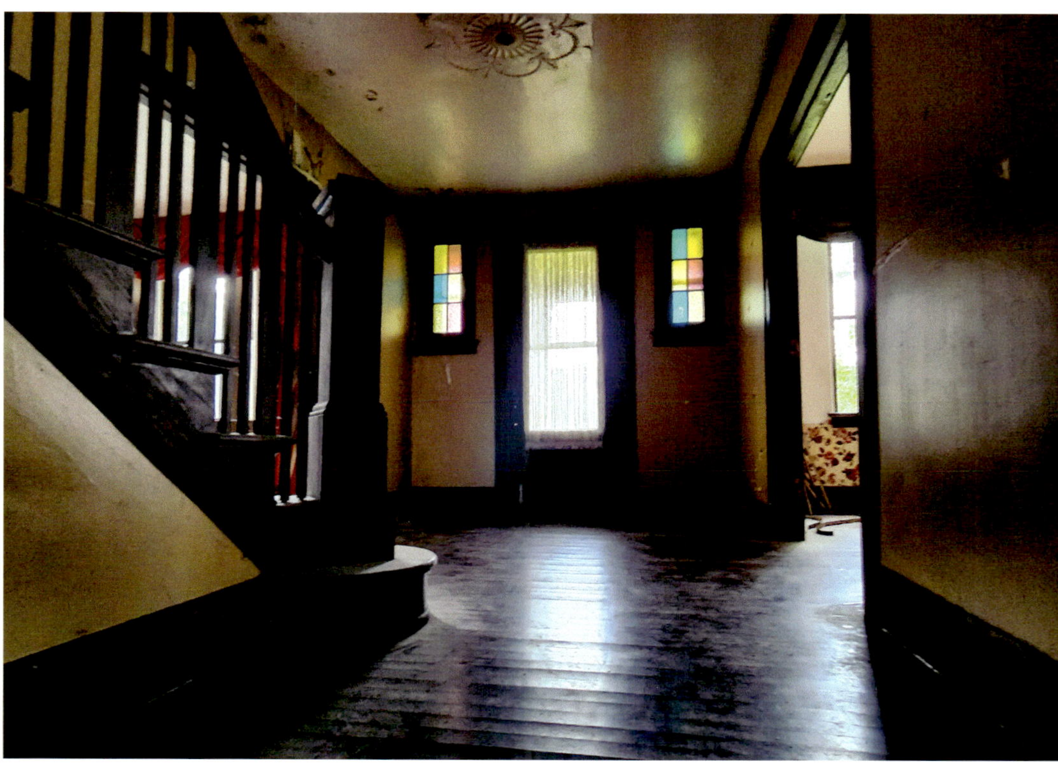

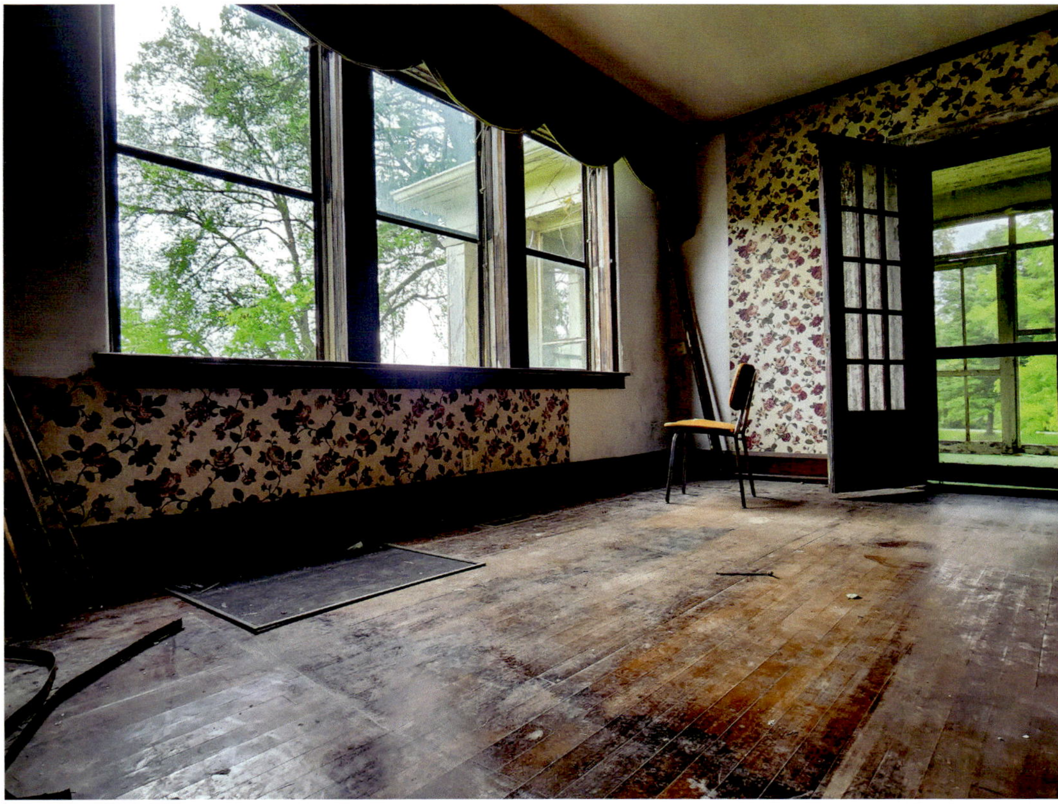

Dining/family room that leads out to the enclosed sunroom.

Opposite above: At this particular institution, the doctors and administrators would also live on the premises. This is one of the doctor's bungalows.

Opposite below: Inside one of the doctor's houses; it was a pleasant surprise to find the stained glass still completely intact.

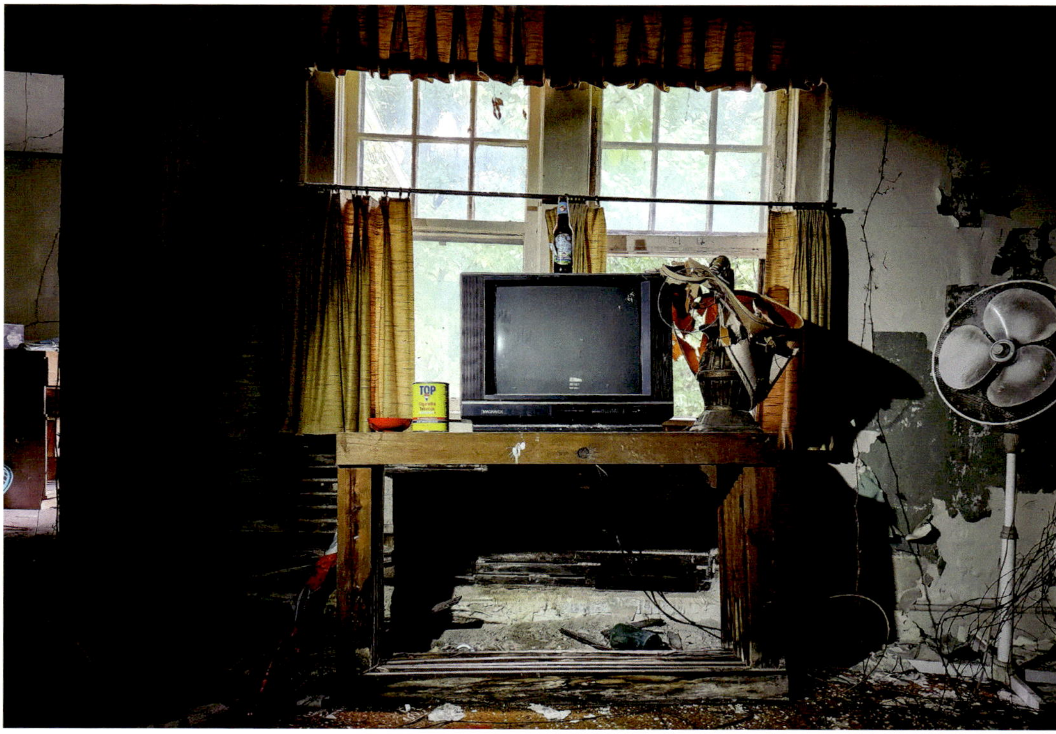

Living room with everything left behind. The beer bottle is most likely from teenagers.

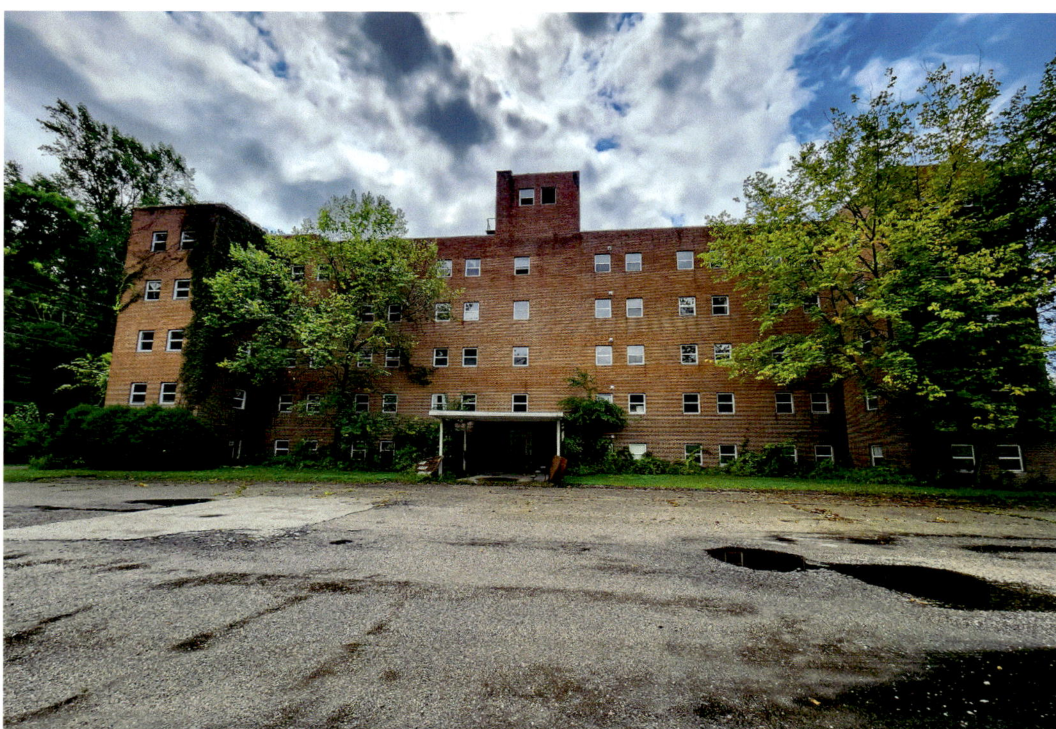

The "new" building, which would become Lee Alan Bryant.

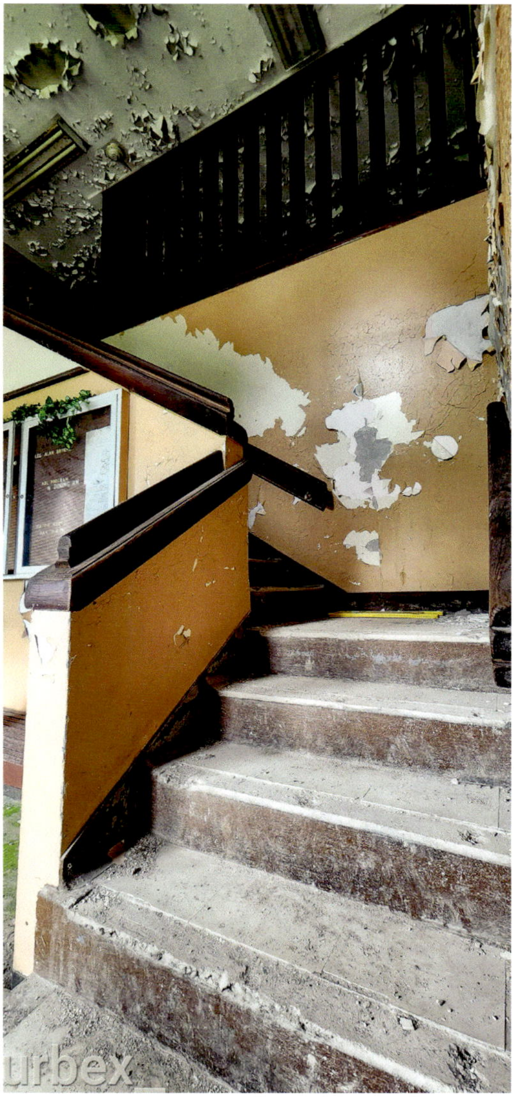

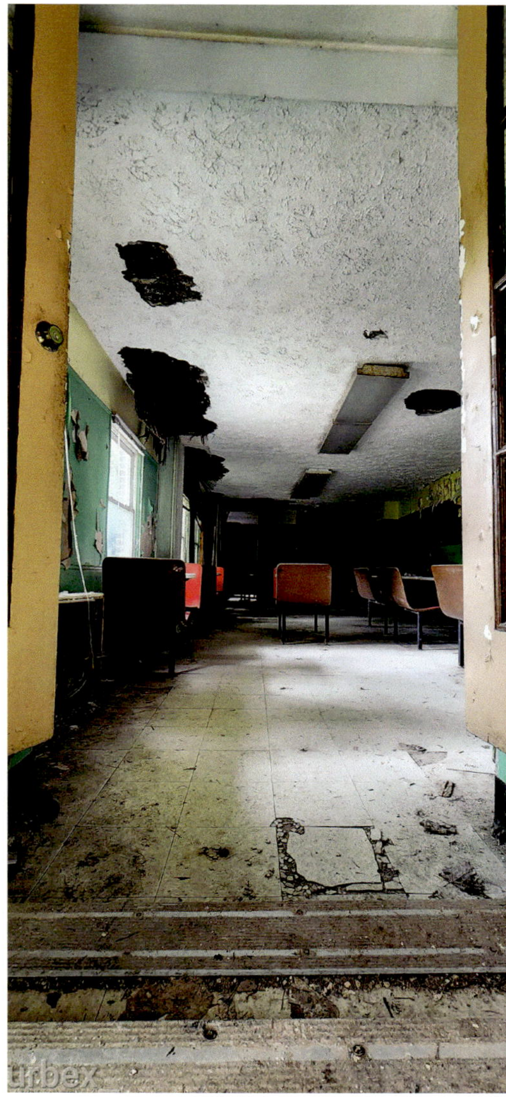

Above left: Staircase in the front foyer. There is also a letter board where messages would be displayed.

Above right: The dining room in this building was set up like a restaurant.

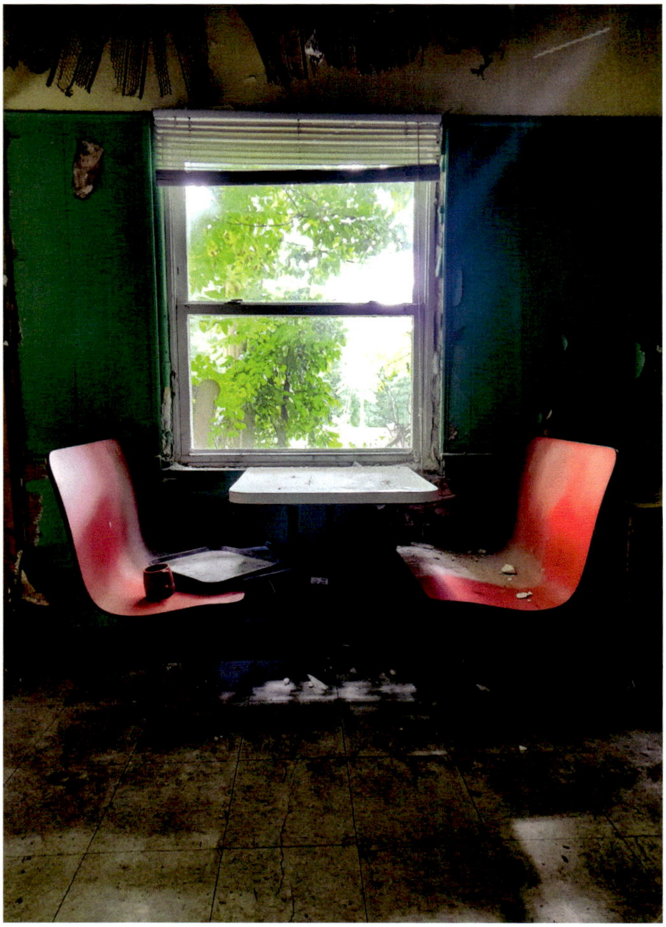

Left: One of the prime location booths, right in front of the window.

Below: A chess game ready to be played.

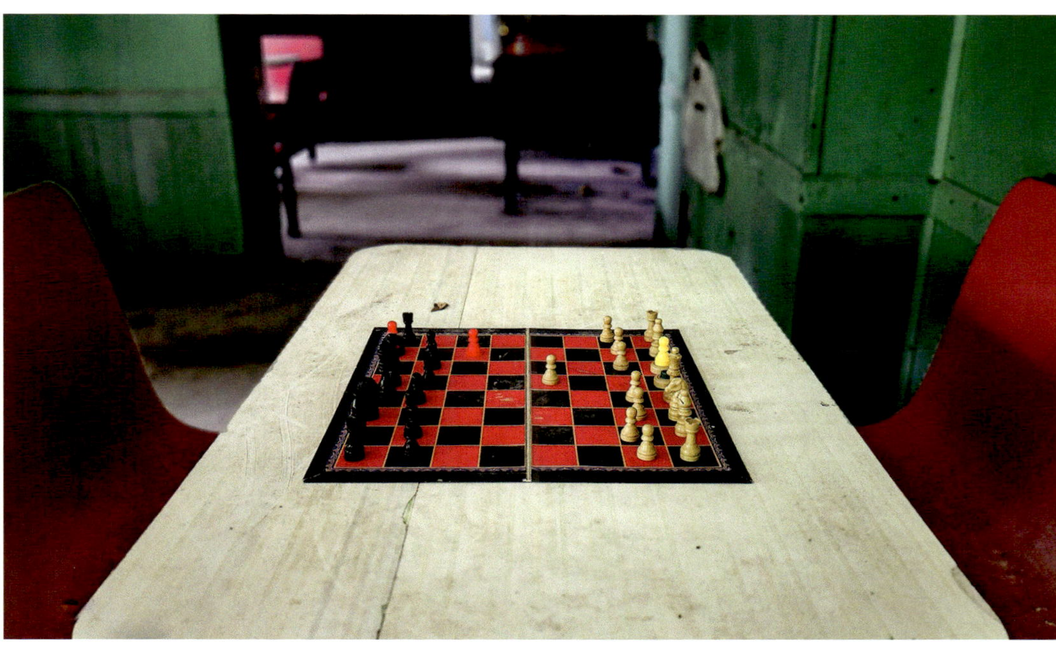

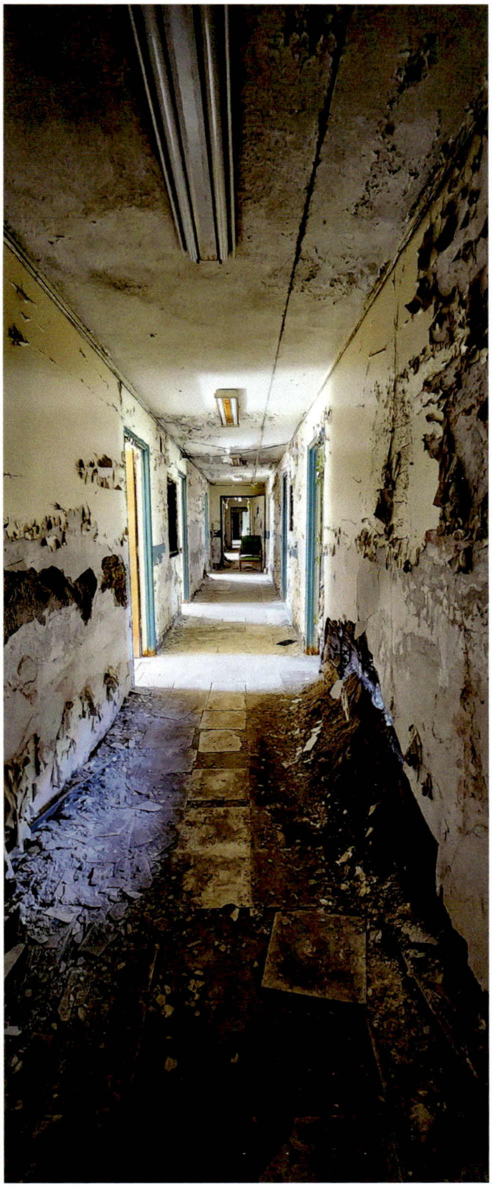

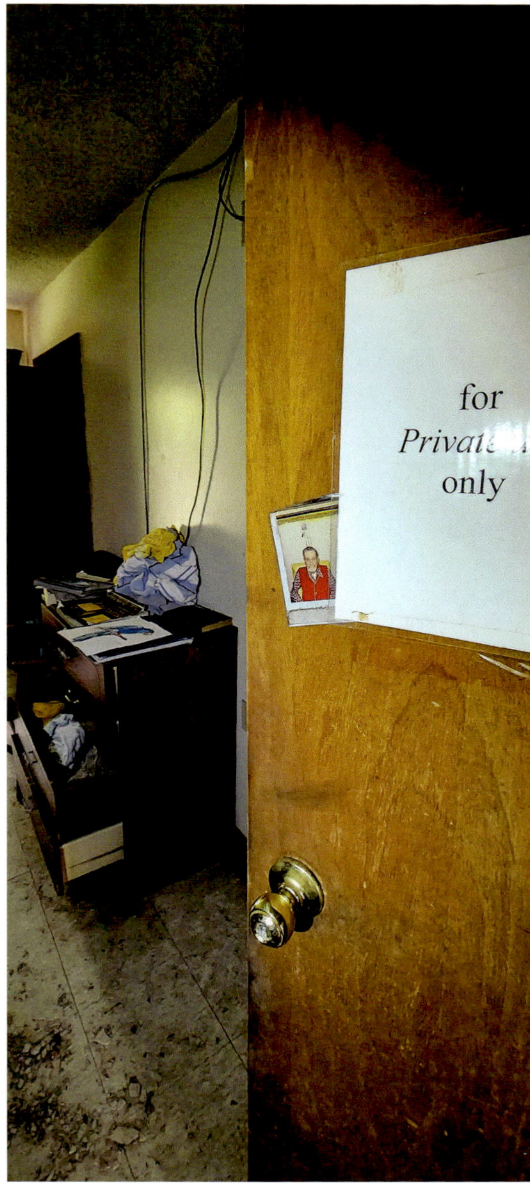

Above left: In the second-floor hallway, it was a welcome surprise that the lights still had their bulbs.

Above right: In the resident room, the drawers still contain personal effects, and the door has a polaroid left on it.

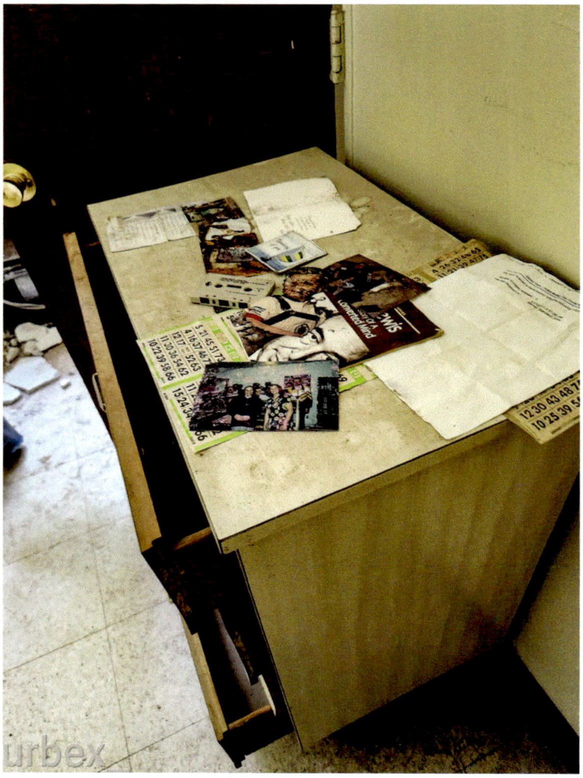

I always find forgotten photos to be so sad, like someone just up and left behind their entire life.

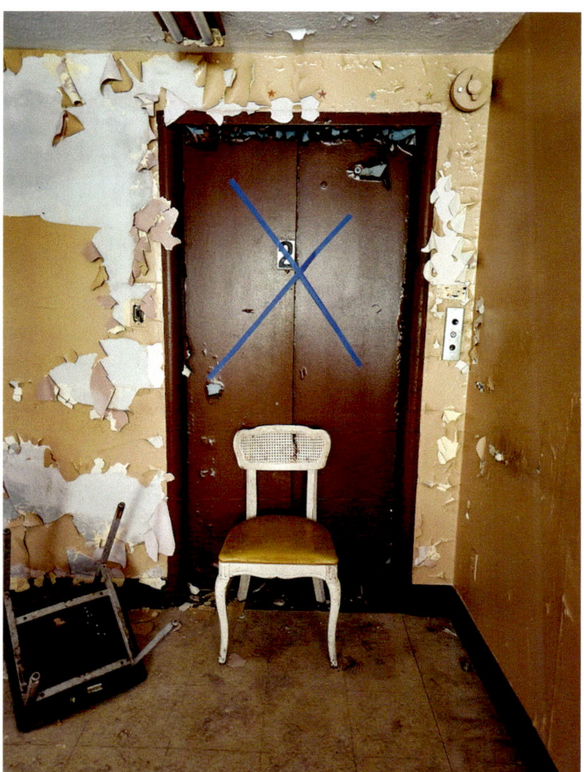

In the second-floor elevator, I like that the brown paint is peeling away to reveal the vibrant teal underneath.

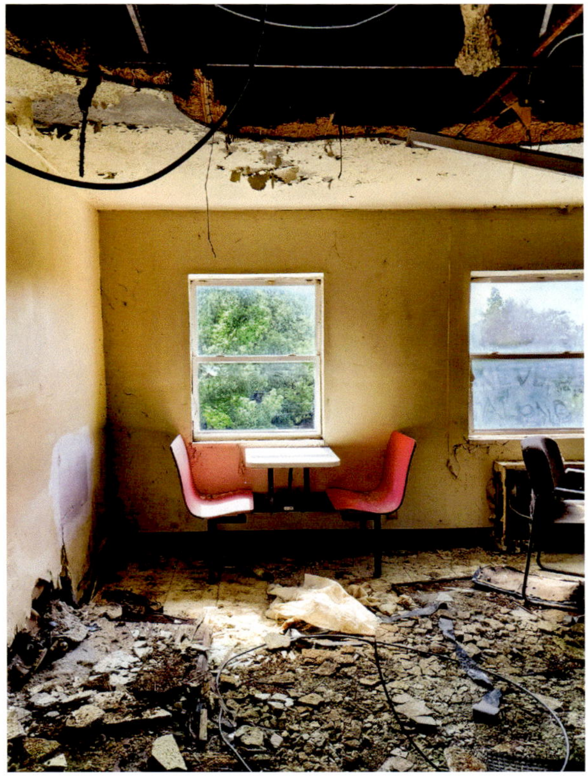

Every floor had a small alcove with at least two booths for a recreation/common area.

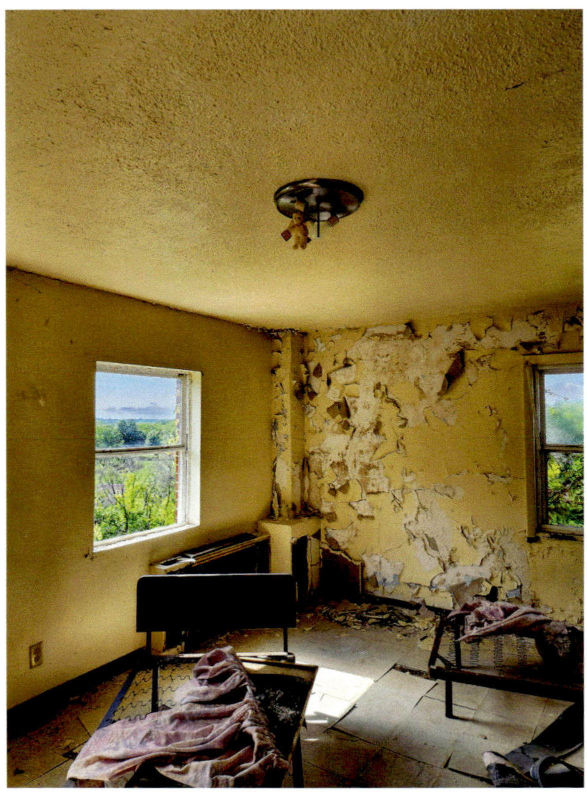

Resident room featuring two beds and bedding.

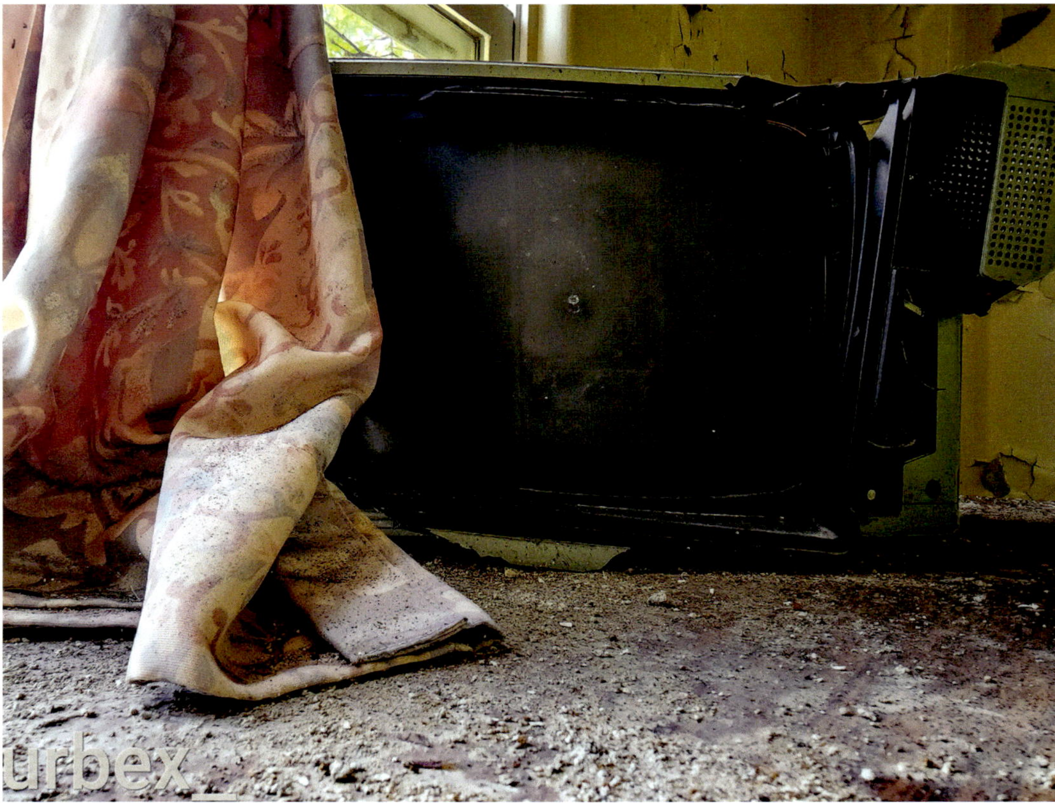

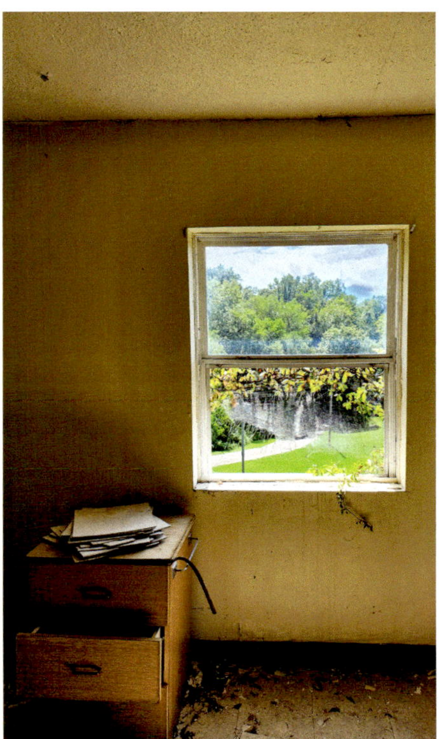

Above: Television left behind in one of the third-floor rooms.

Left: Third-floor resident room that still had a night stand (with tiles left on top).

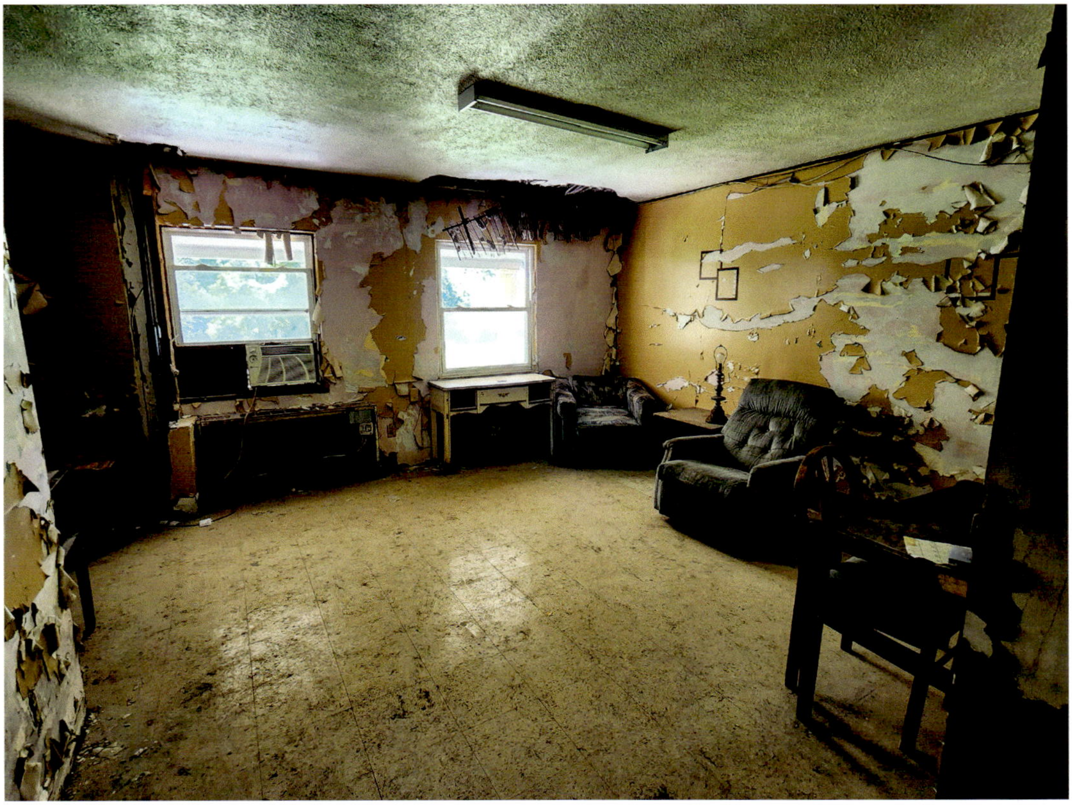

Above: This was one of the bigger rooms in the building. It had two recliners and two desks.

Right: A lonely chair photo, because no exploration is complete without one, especially a chair as regal as this one.

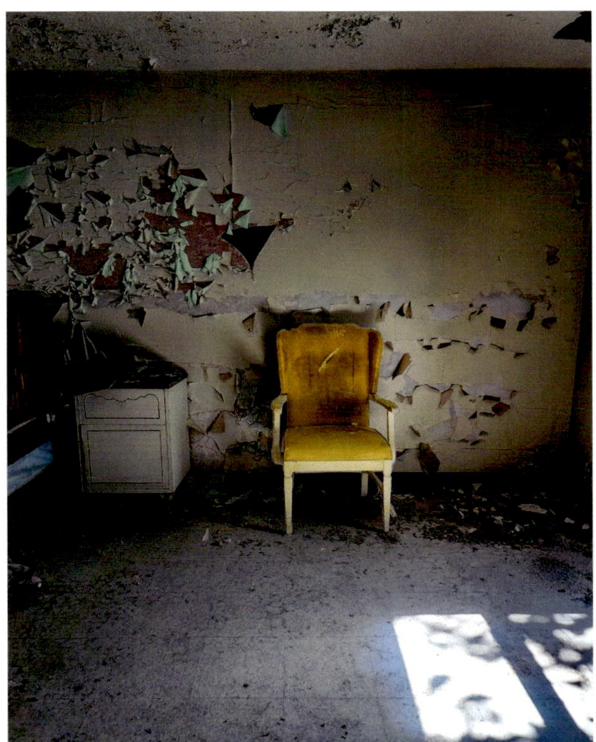

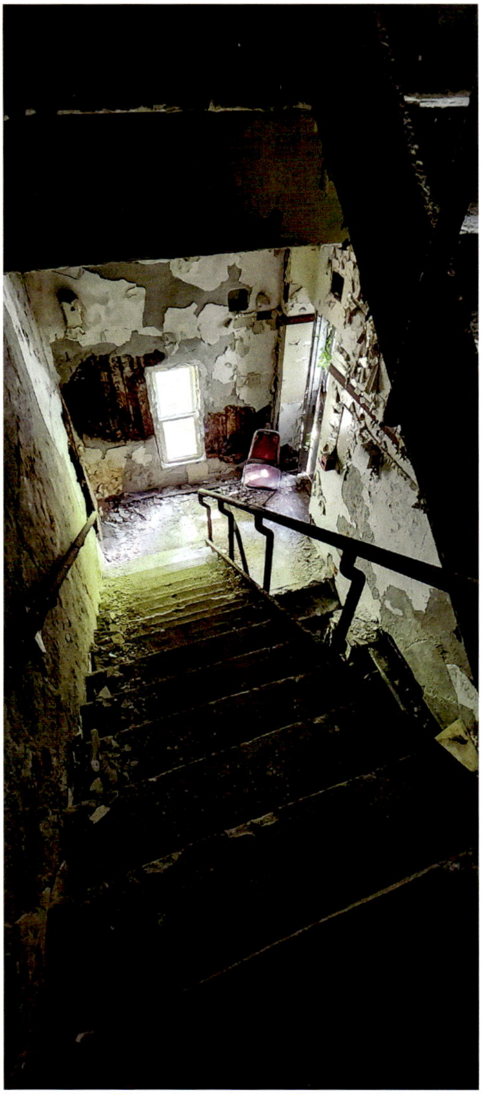

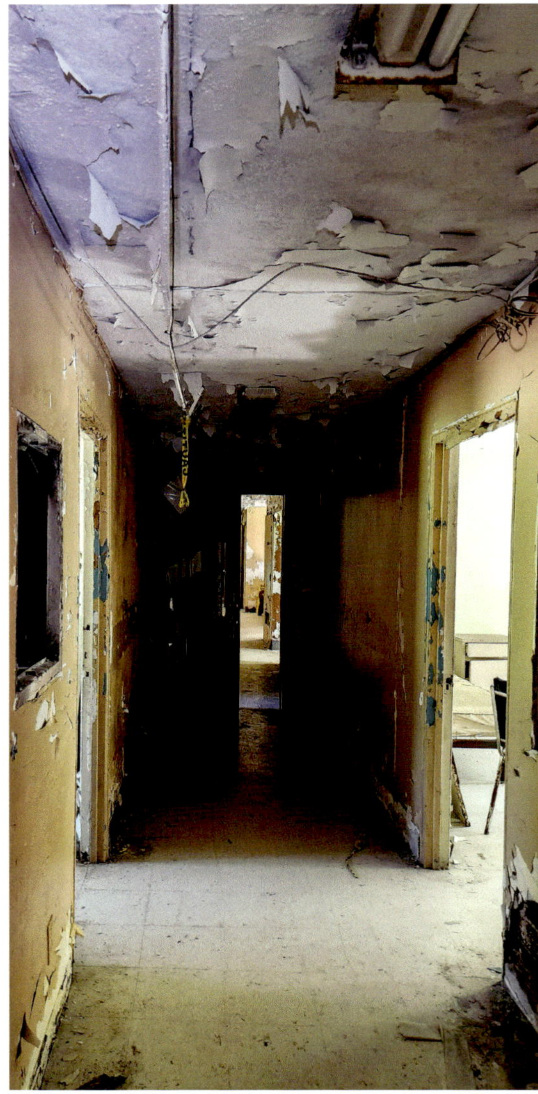

Above left: The stairway to go back down to the main level.

Above right: Third-floor hallway, with beige paint chipping away to reveal some beautiful teal.

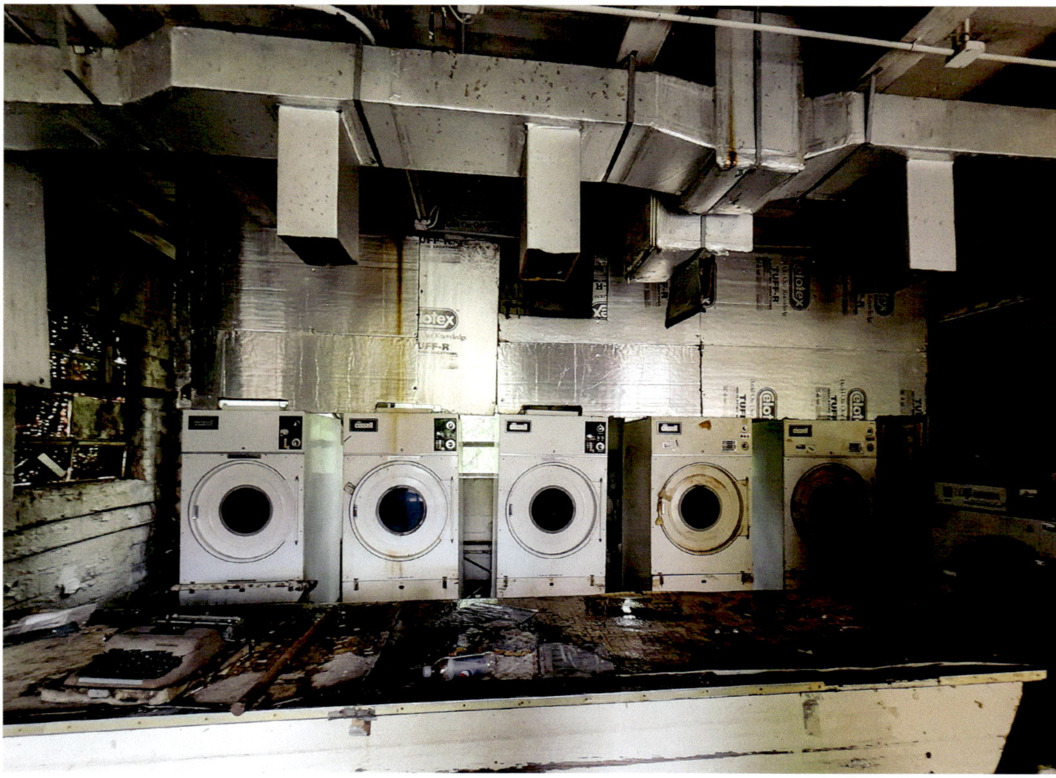

Above: Laundry room, which is semi-connected to the original building.

Right: A typewriter left behind in the laundry room.

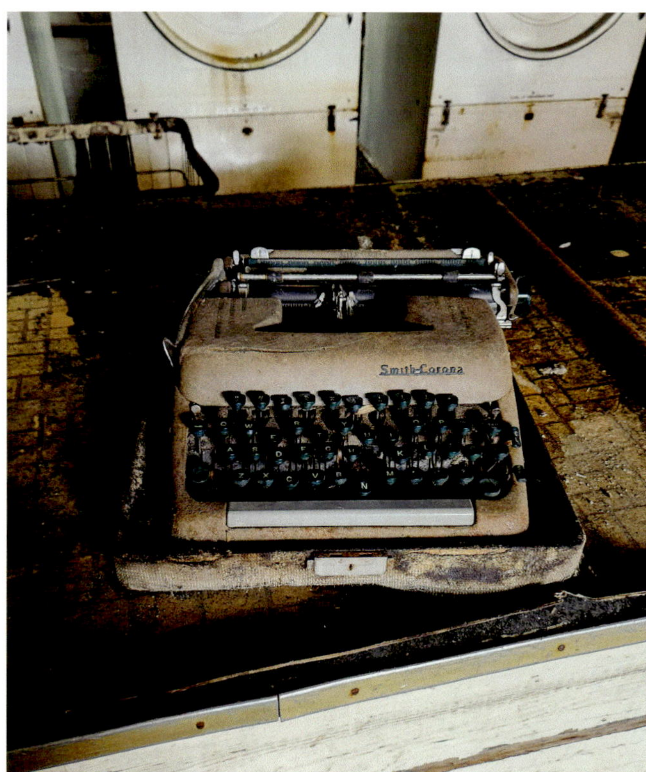

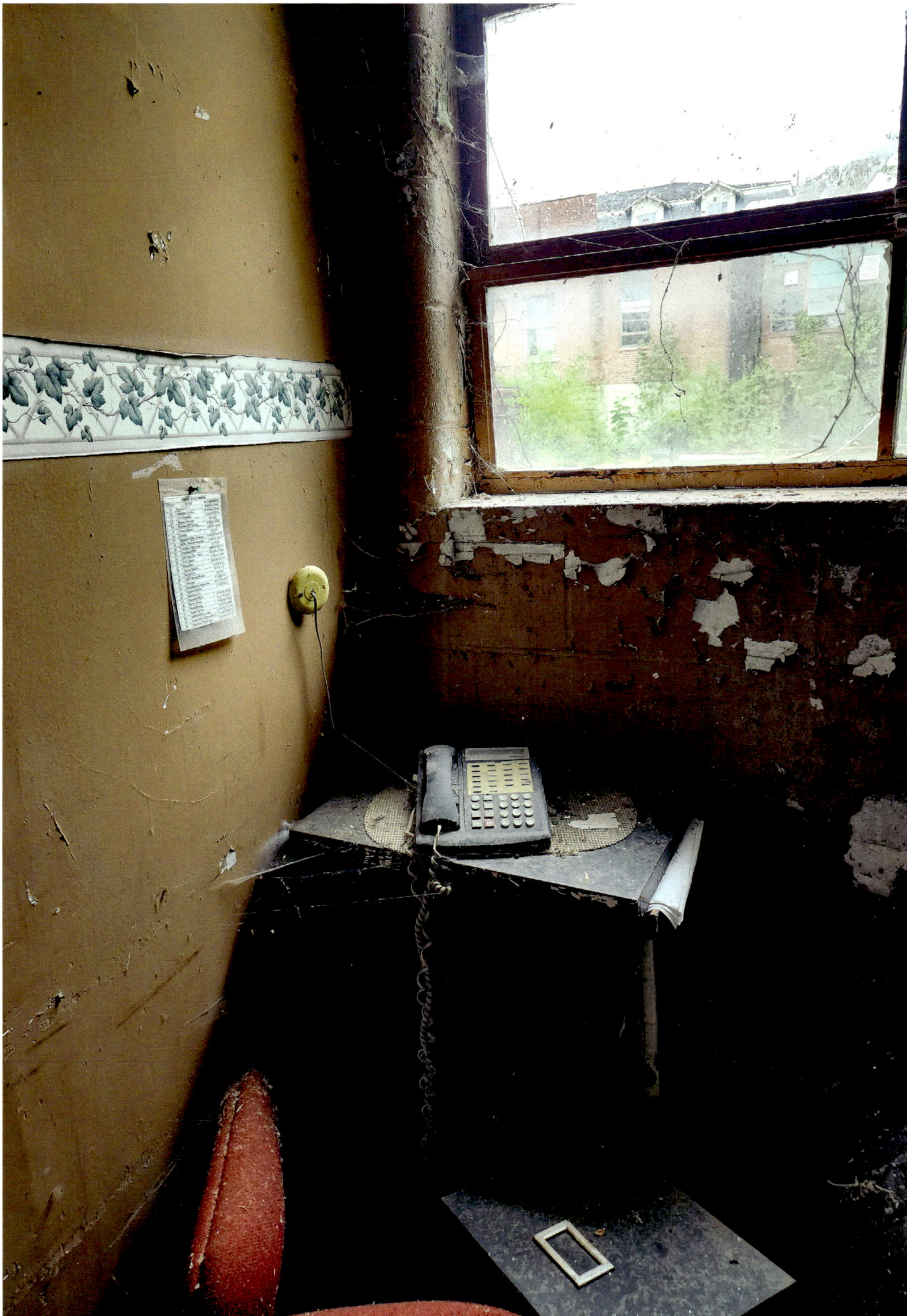

The phone nook has a chair, a list of extensions, and of course, a phone.

4

NEWPORT CHEMICAL DEPOT

The Newport Chemical Depot (NECD) was a 6,990-acre bulk chemical storage and destruction facility managed by the United States Army. It was opened in 1941 as the Wabash River Ordnance Works, later known as the Newport Army Ammunition Plant, and was one of nine Army chemical weapons storage facilities in the United States. The location was used to manufacture solid explosives such as trinitrotoluene and RDX, as well as heavy water. When the nerve toxin VX was in use, it also functioned as the production site for all of the U.S. military's nerve agents. The area was chosen due to labor availability, access to a railroad line, electric power and water, and its remote location. In addition, the location must be at least 200 miles away from attack. Because there was an acute demand for RDX, the factory was built to mimic the Woolwich process. The government purchased 21,986 acres from sixty-two landowners for the plant. There were sixty-six clusters of buildings, six cemeteries, and one church among the farmland. As of 1998, the cemeteries, one of which appeared to date from 1810, were still being maintained. Construction began on January 12, 1942, with production beginning on July 20, 1942. The plant closed in 1946, but it was reopened in 1951 to produce RDX for the Korean War.

The Newport Army Ammunition Facility constructed a heavy water plant in 1943–1944. It was utilized to make heavy water for the U.S. nuclear weapons program in the 1950s. The Army constructed a VX facility at the location in 1959. The Newport Army Chemical Plant was the name of the facility. The Newport Army Ammunition Plant was formed in 1964 when the Wabash River Ordnance Works and the Newport Army Chemical Plant merged and were renamed the Newport Army Ammunition Plant. Newport became a chemical weapons manufacturing center in 1961, generating the entire U.S. stockpile of VX nerve toxin. It was then utilized to store and eventually neutralize the remaining 1,269 short tons of chemical weapons that remained after the United States' chemical weapons program was halted and transit prohibited.

Over 675 jobs were lost when Newport Chemical Depot was shut down as recommended by the 2005 Base Realignment and Closure Commission. The Depot had been the biggest employer in rural Vermillion County, which had around 16,000 residents. Over 1,000 people were present when the VX agent was neutralized. After the base's closure was announced, leaders from the local, regional, and state levels met with members of the public to plan how to rehabilitate the depot. The Newport Chemical Depot Redevelopment Authority (NeCDRA), made up of residents of the area, was established as a result. Three committees were set up by the NeCDRA during the planning process to research and offer recommendations on land use, infrastructure, and economic growth. The reuse plan's four criteria—job creation, high environmental standards, fiscal responsibility, and economic viability—were supported in part because views from all sectors were heard. The plan includes spaces for industry and technology, as well as parks, open space, natural regions, and areas used for agriculture and forestry. Additionally, there is a location set aside for conservation activities that protect a bat species that is in risk of extinction

As of 2022, there are spaces open for new businesses to move to Vermillion Rise Park.

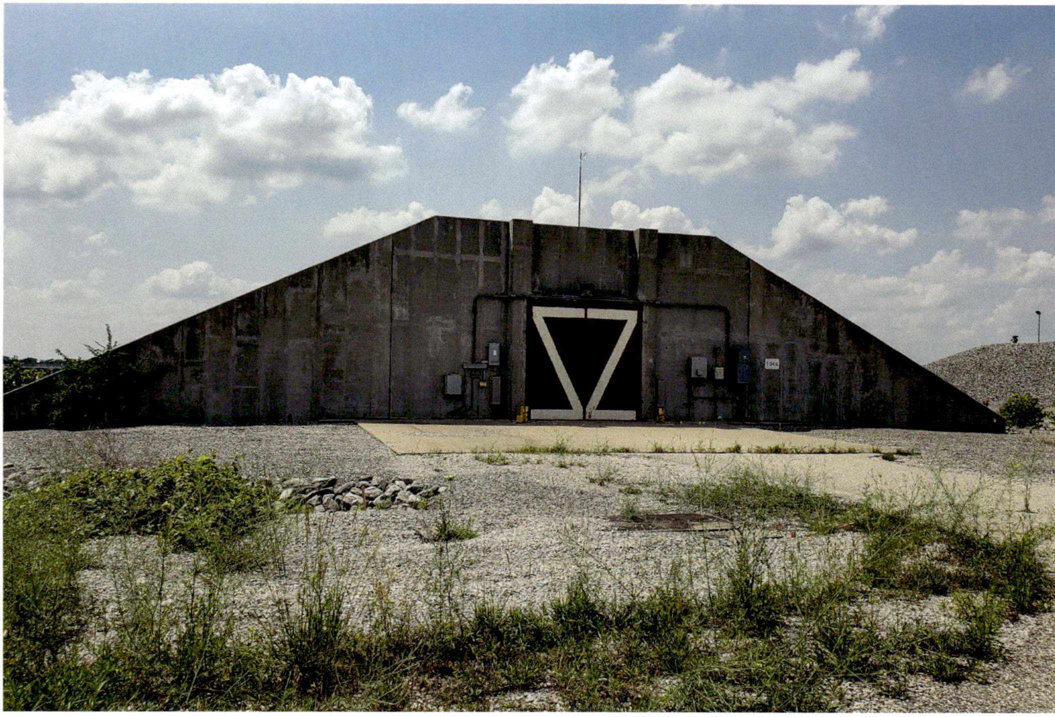

One of the bunkers that at one time held VX nerve gas.

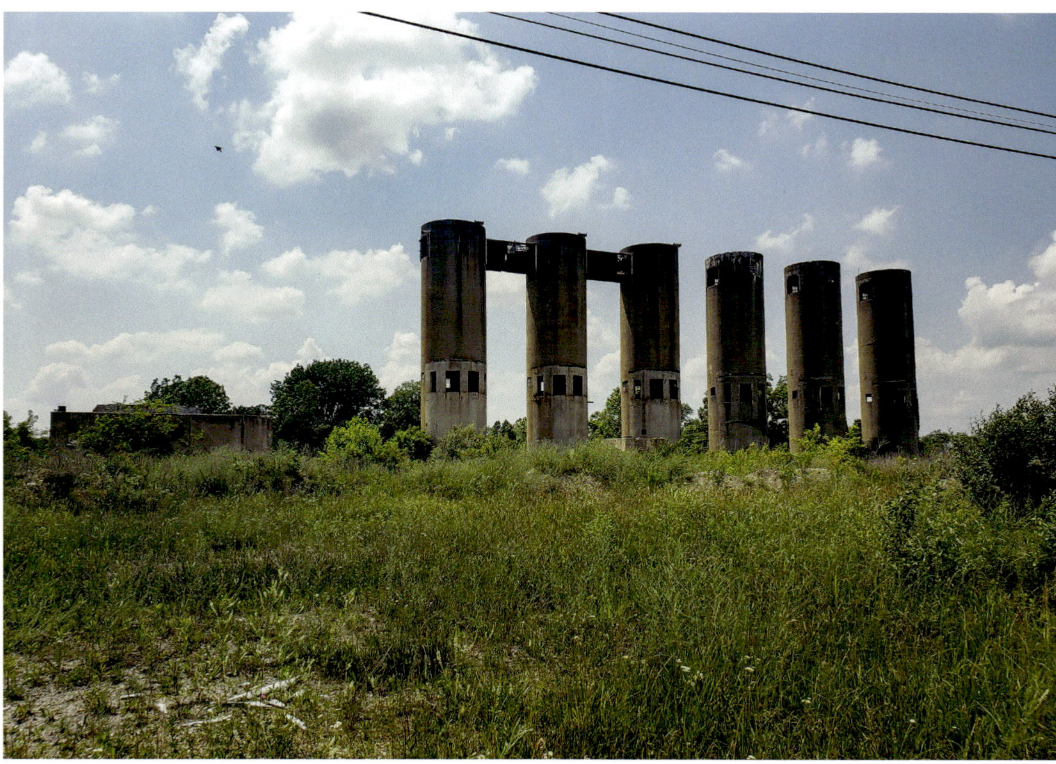

These towers would have held chemicals.

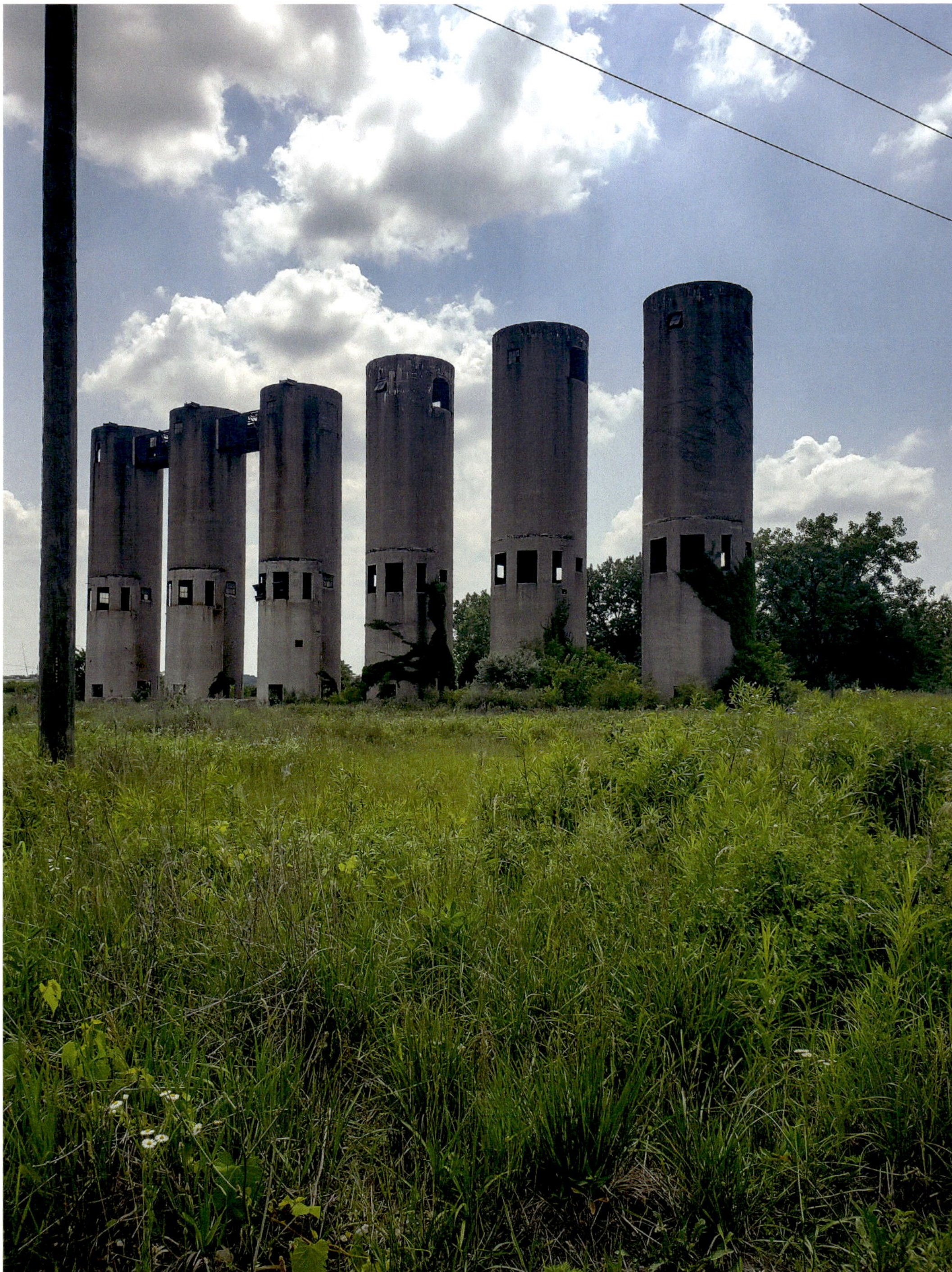

Another shot of the towers.

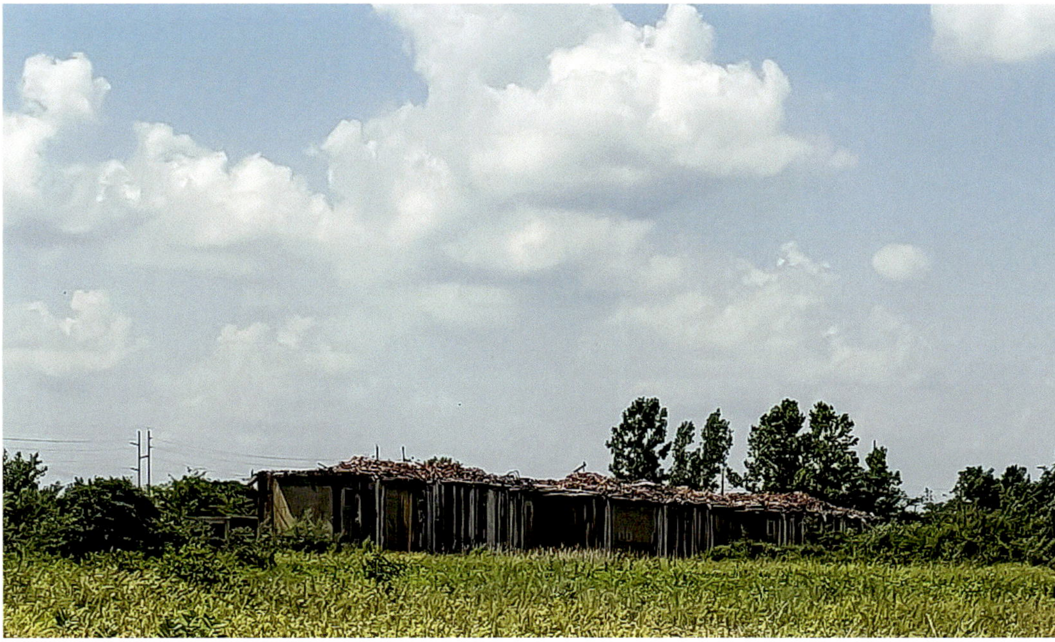

Above: After being decommissioned and purchased by private parties, many of the buildings are in ruins.

Right: One of the high security buildings, which still has the alarm attached.

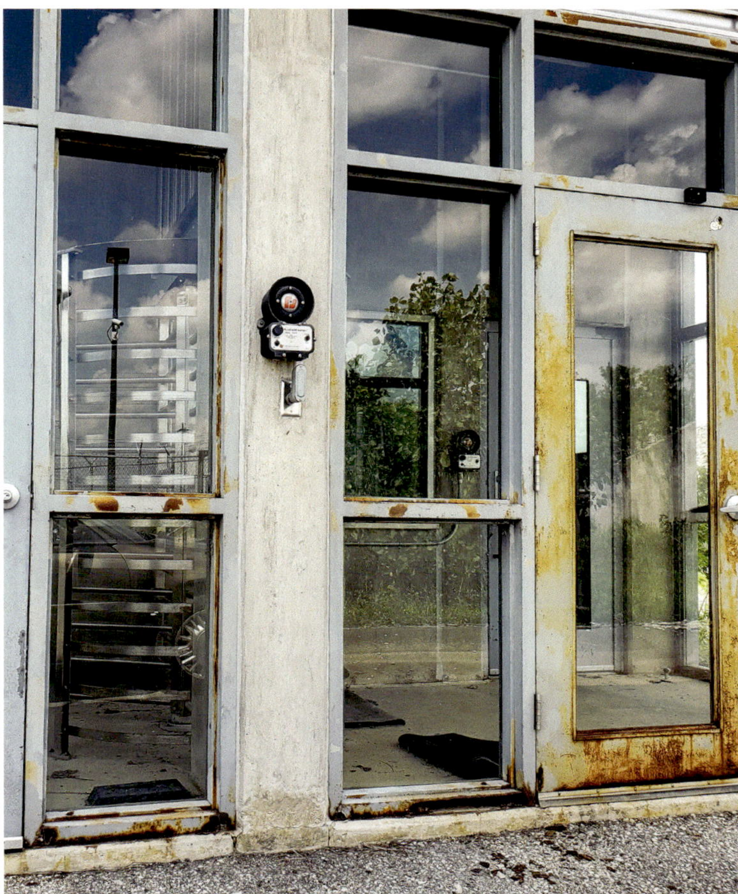

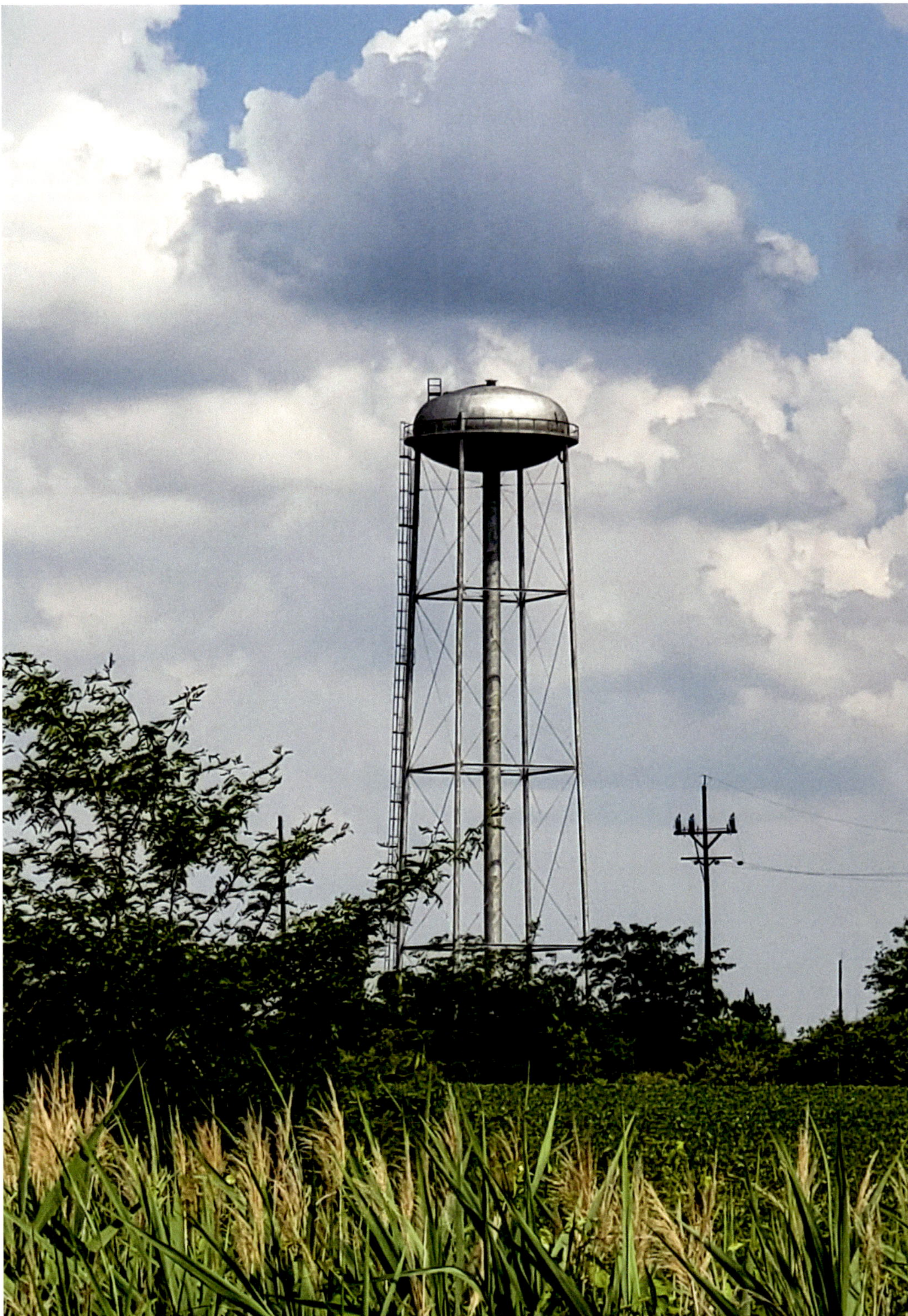

I absolutely loved the water tower.

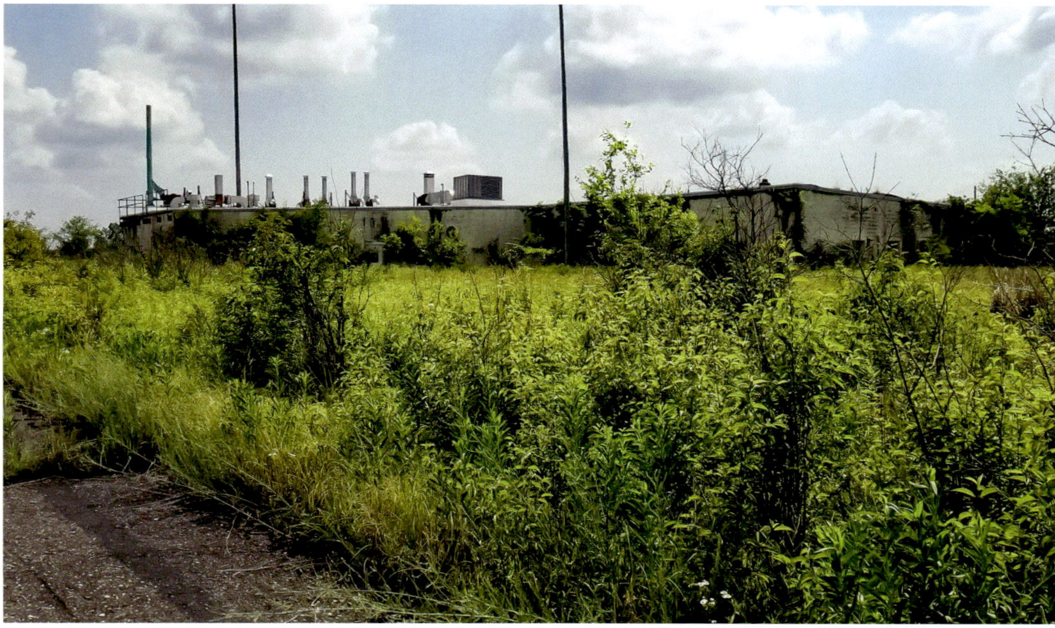

Above: The remains of one of the factories.

Right: A smaller building attached to the factory. One of the stipulations of us being allowed into this location was to not get out of the car, so many of the photos are long distance shots.

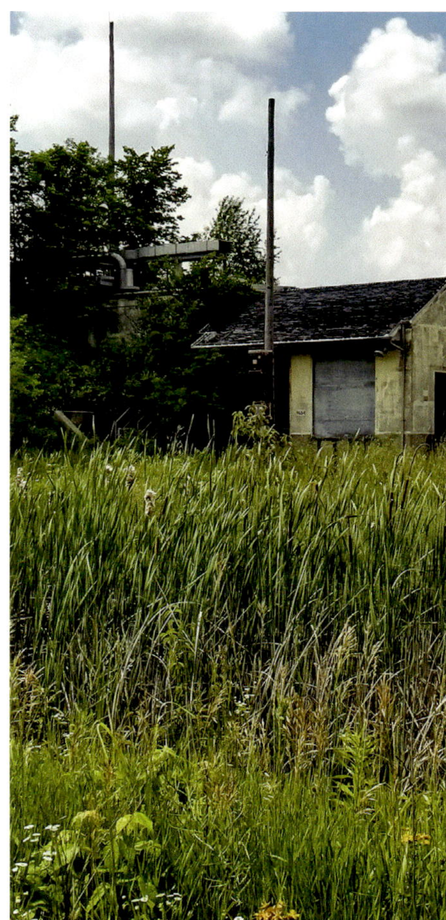

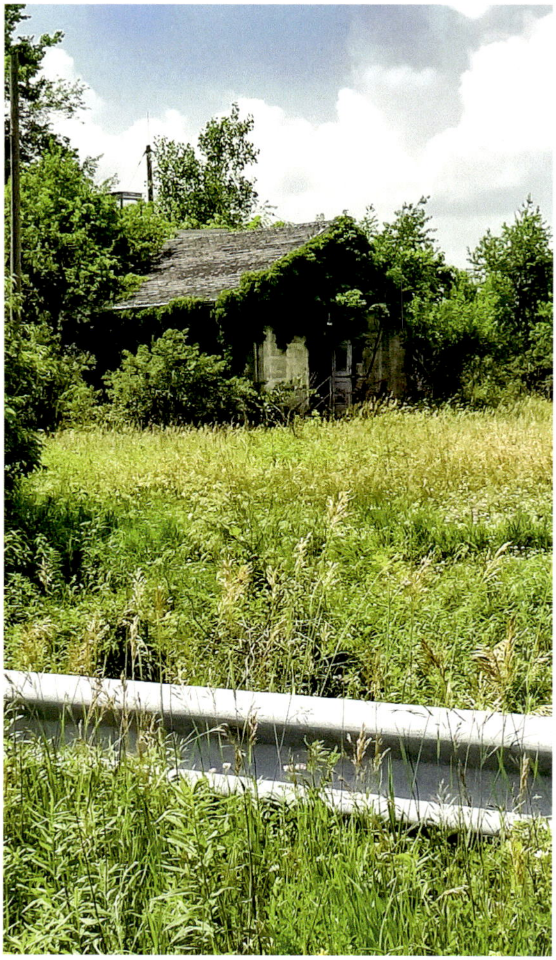

Left: A different small building with its doors left open. This location was big enough that we had to use Google maps to navigate around.

Below: A different bunker that is still in fantastic condition.

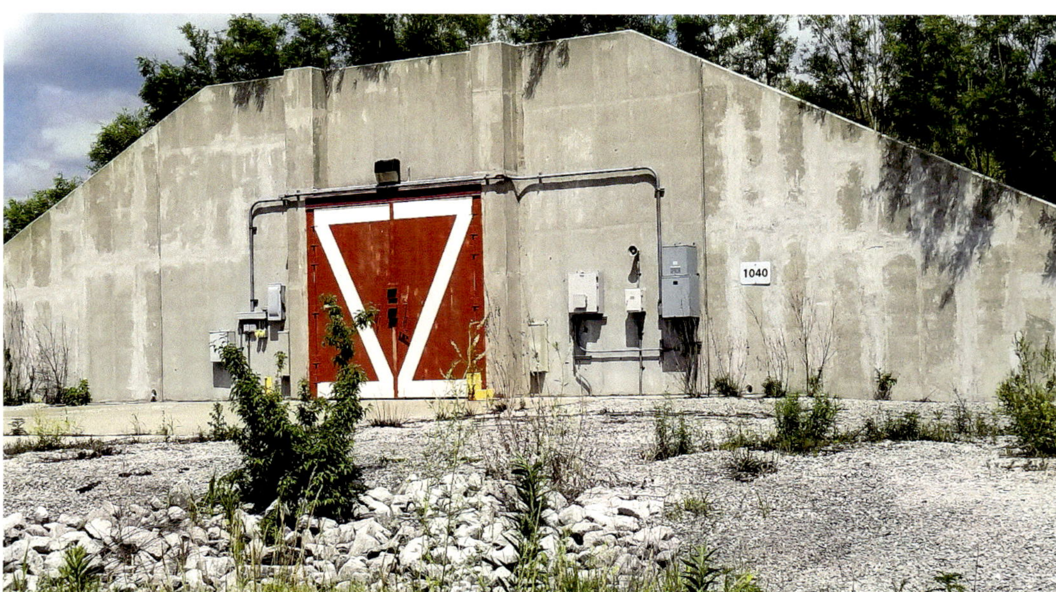

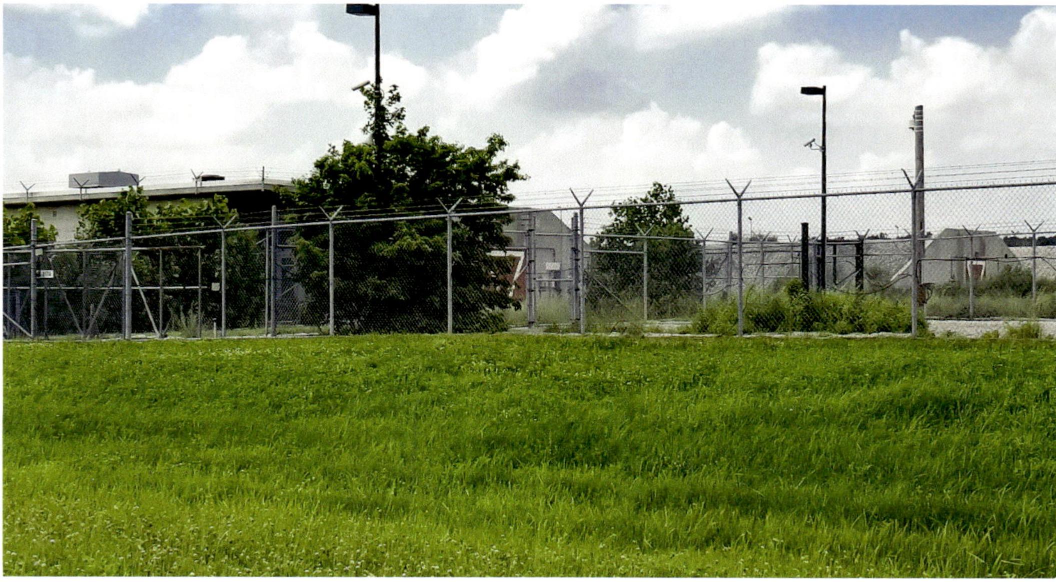

Above: A razor wire topped fence surrounded this entire area.

Right: Parts of the industrial complex that has been left to decay in a field.

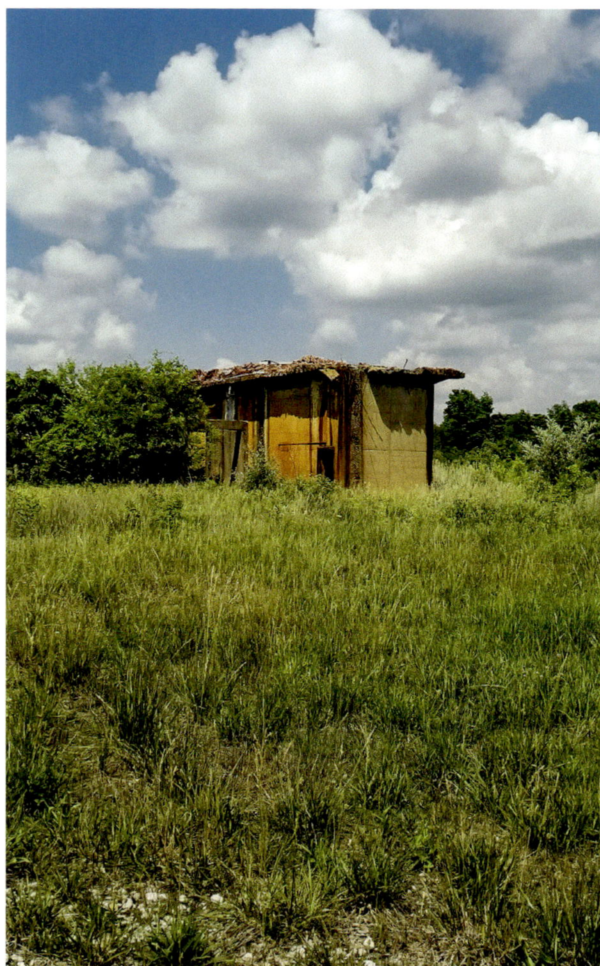

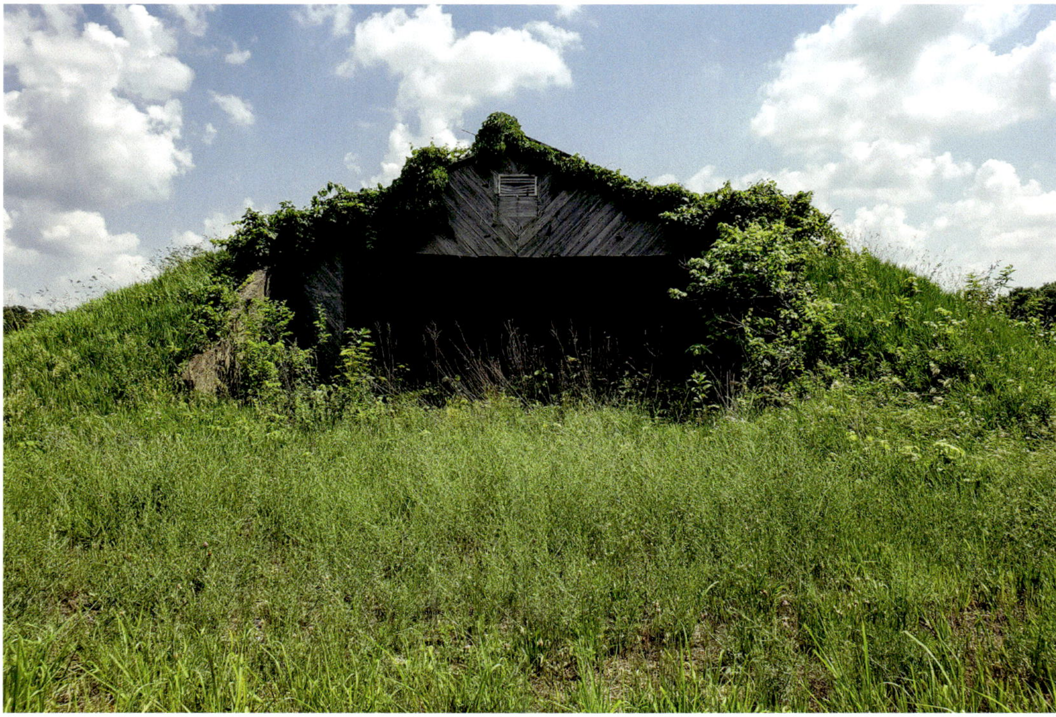

Most of the sheds in this area were hidden under foliage, which was a common way to camouflage things during that time period.

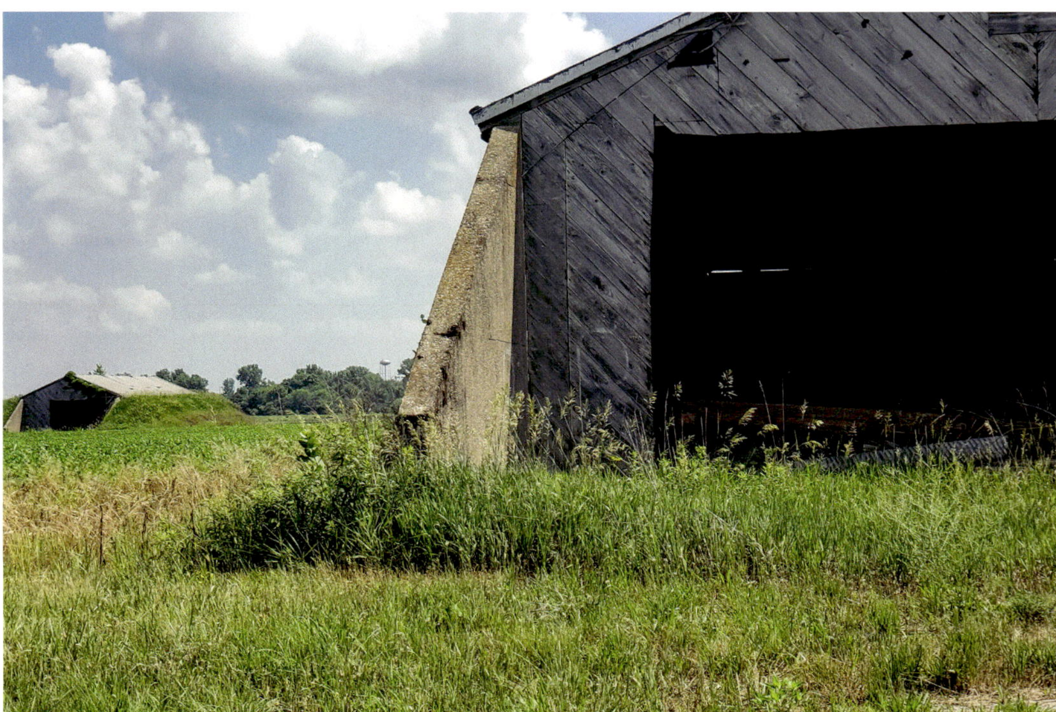

Some of them have become uncovered over the years, but there is still a vast amount left behind.

5

THUNDER ISLAND WATERPARK

On the outskirts of Westfield, Indiana, Thunder Island, a once-bustling small-town water park that first opened in 1975, is now deserted. The waterpark, which is miles from the main road and only accessible on foot from a small parking lot next to a cemetery, is somewhat of a local legend that is mostly forgotten by everyone but the most intrepid people. Despite the fact that Thunder Island was forced to close in 1993 for financial reasons, persistent tales about a grisly fatality on one of the waterslides have not been dispelled (Mitchell).

The 3-J Family Recreation Center on 16 acres of property at Westfield's Thunder Island first opened its doors in 1975; however, at that time there were no water-related activities available there. It wasn't until the facility's expansion in 1984 that the proprietors added water attractions like the Raging Rapids tube ride and three water slides—the Shark, Stingray, and Barracuda—to increase daytime traffic. Additionally, Thunder Island 3-J Family Recreation was given a name change. In addition to the swimming amenities, the park featured bumper boats, go-karts, a miniature golf course, batting cages for baseball and softball, volleyball courts, and an arcade. It's plausible that Thunder Island was ahead of its time. Pools were wonderful for the competitive swimmer, but the idea of inner-tube rides and water slides was starting to catch on with people looking for a little more excitement when it came to getting out of the summer heat.

Thunder Island made a brief appearance in the 1990 film, *Freeze Frame*, which starred Shannen Doherty from *Beverly Hills 90210*. Doherty plays a high school journalist who uncovers a political scandal with her news crew and is pursued across Indianapolis by bad guys until they meet up at a waterslide at Thunder Island. The movie was shot in the fall of 1988. In 1994, Thunder Island Water and

Recreation Park—the park's final official name—filed for Chapter 11 bankruptcy with the intention of reopening. Owner Mike Maio was reportedly going through a personal bankruptcy at the time, according to news sources. (Mitchell) The personal bankruptcy was the result of Maio being convicted of insider trading, along with Louis P. Ferrero and. Patricia Ladavac. (Securities and Exchange Commission)

In June and July of 1988, Maio and Ladavac both received information from Ferrero, the chairman, president, and chief executive officer of Anacomp, Inc. ("Anacomp"), that Anacomp was in the process of negotiating a tender offer for shares of Xidex Corporation ("Xidex"). Ferrero and Maio first became acquainted in the 1970s through their mutual friend, Dr. Ronald Palamara ("Palamara"), the creator of Anacomp, a sizable publicly traded business with a focus on information services. Maio and Palamara were friends until Palamara's death in 1985; they had grown up together in Indianapolis. Midway through the 1970s, when Ferrero sold his company to Anacomp and started working there, he ran into Palamara. Ferrero gave Maio a loan of $250,000 in 1987 to help him with development costs at an amusement park owned by Maio's family and the Palamara estate, which at the time was in need of money. Even though this was the greatest personal loan Ferrero had ever given, Maio made no commitments about a promissory note, interest payments, or mortgages.

To satisfy the demands of the creditors, 65 acres of the park were sold in portions to a consortium of private investors for $2.2 million. The property has been the subject of numerous attempts to redevelop it over the years, but none of them have been successful. Maio passed away in June 2019, and the following winter, Chatham Hills LLP bought the property where Thunder Island formerly stood and began dismantling its remnants. As of 2022, the project has halted. (Mitchell)

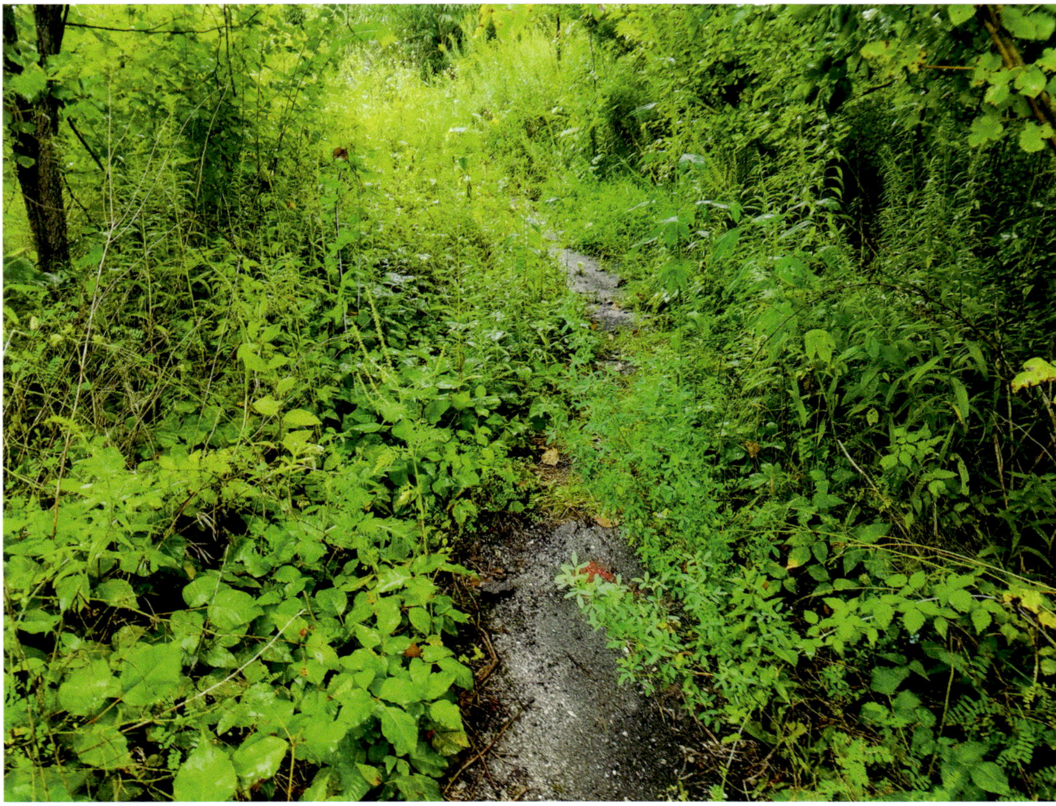

Above: Most of the sidewalk to get into the park had been taken over by foliage, except for this one small strip.

Right: Standing in what was once the parking lot, there is still a for sale sign, and you can see one of the highways next to it.

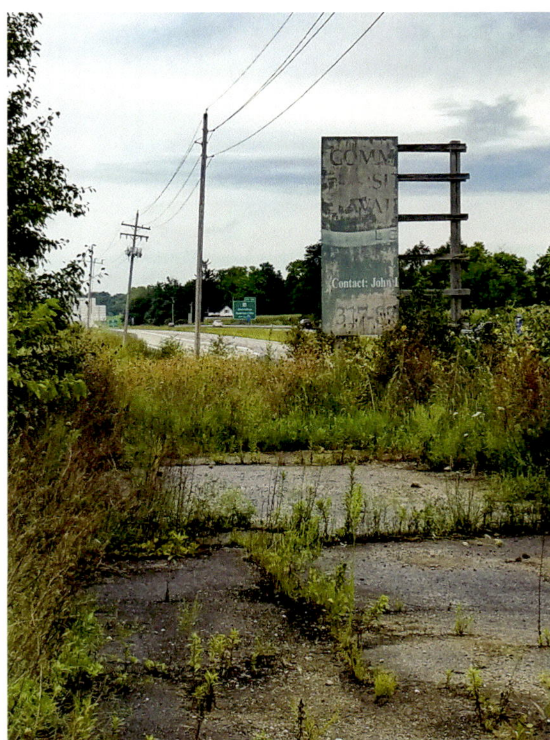

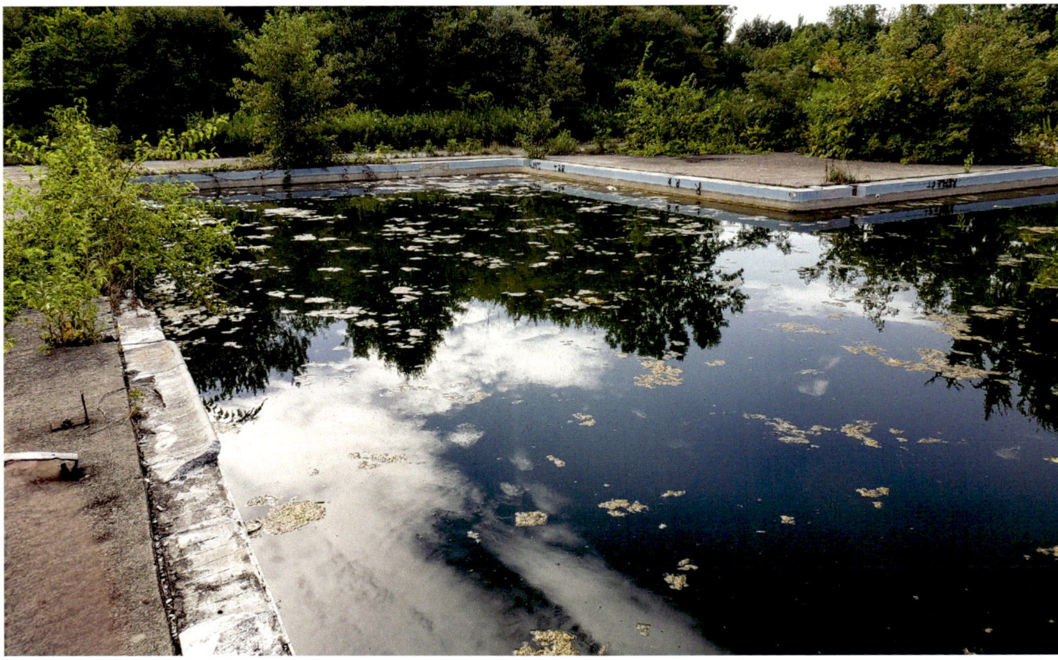

This was the first pool you would see when you made to the actual park, after walking through the woods for twenty minutes.

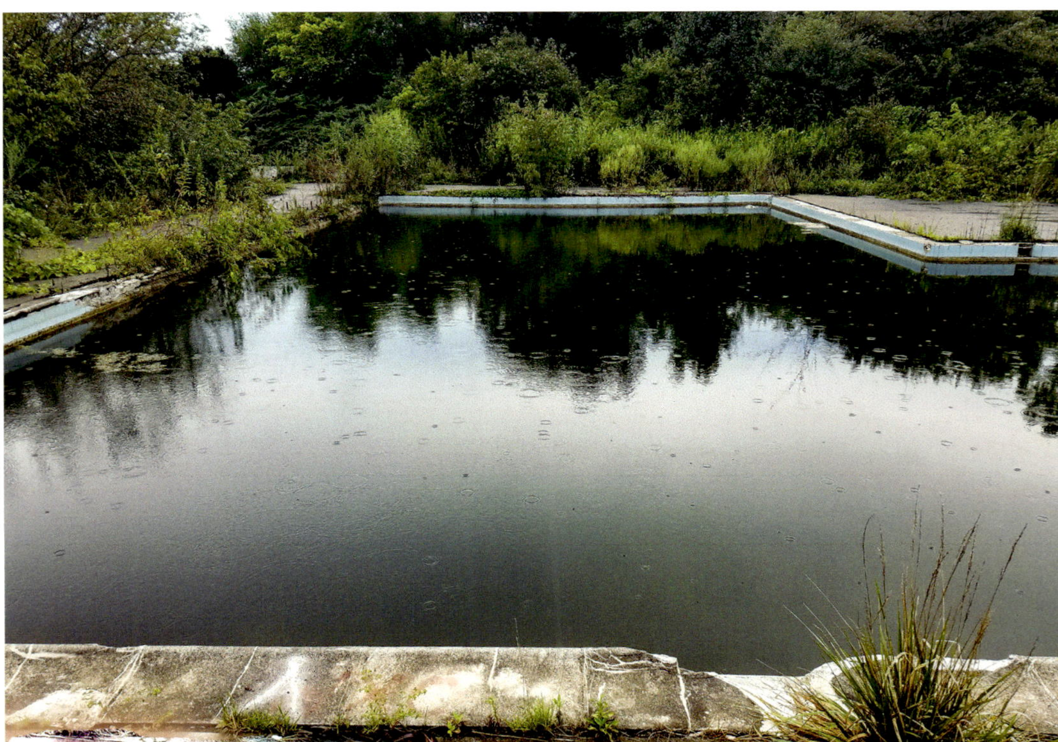

This was the biggest pool we saw. It had been reclaimed by mosquitoes and small turtles, which definitely startled me a few times.

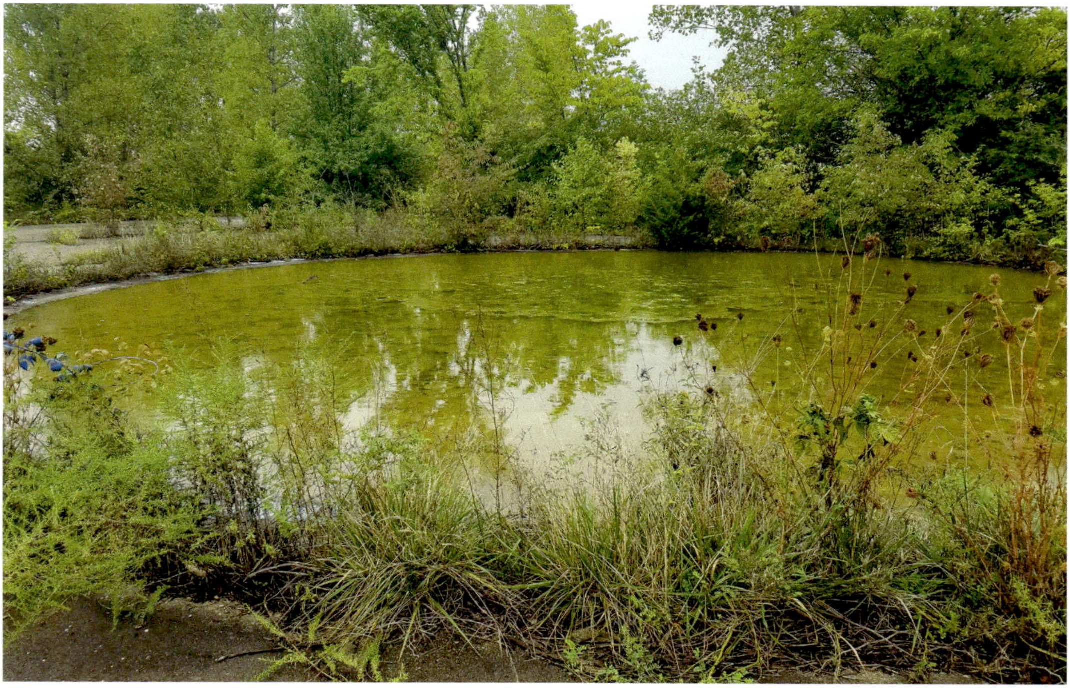

A wading pool, which is full of algae and other plant life.

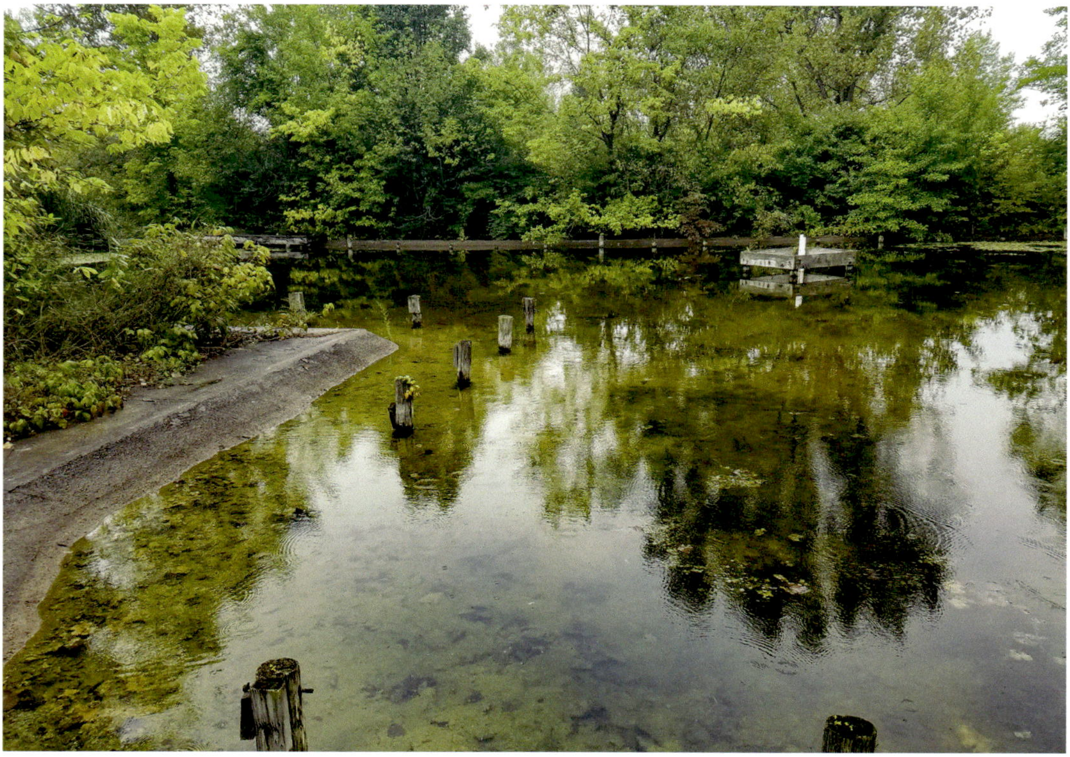

This pool was connected to one of the large slides that were an attraction.

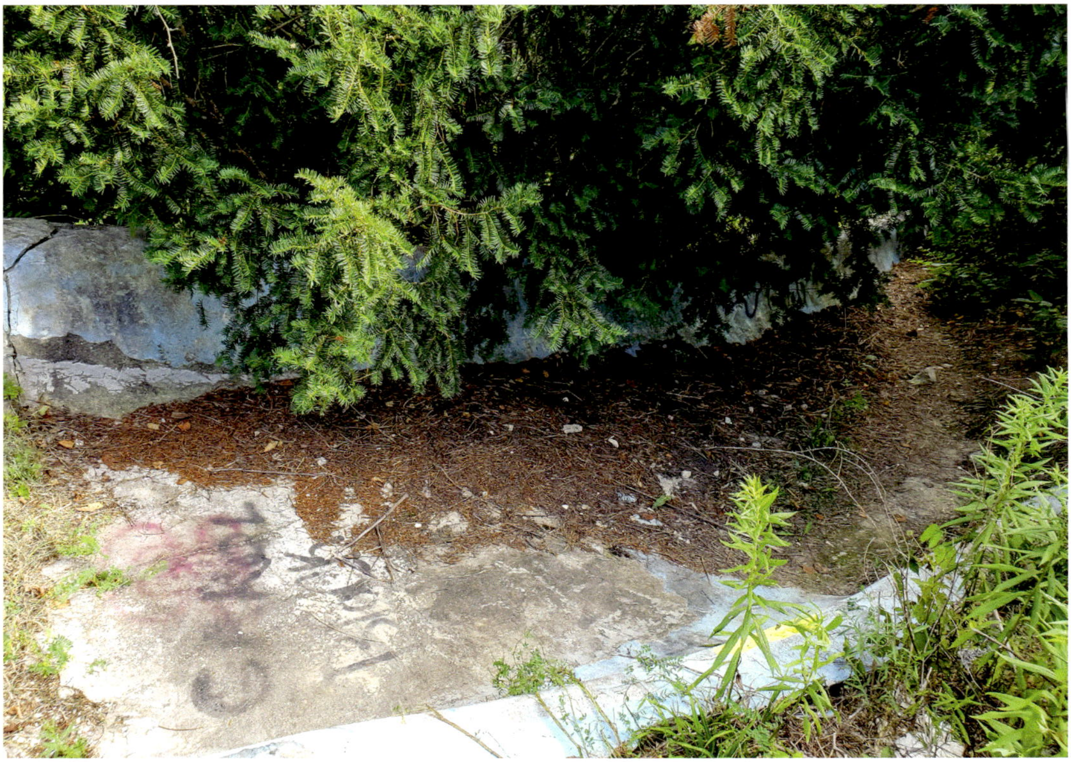

Part of the slide that is still visible through the underbrush.

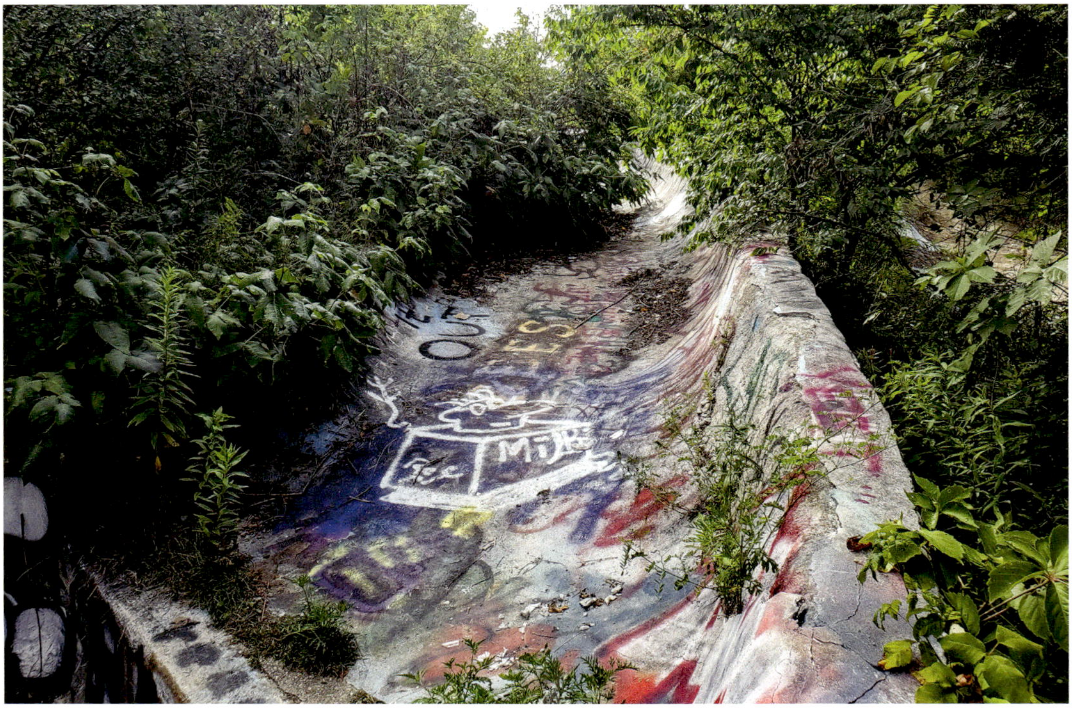

More of the slide taken further up a small hill.

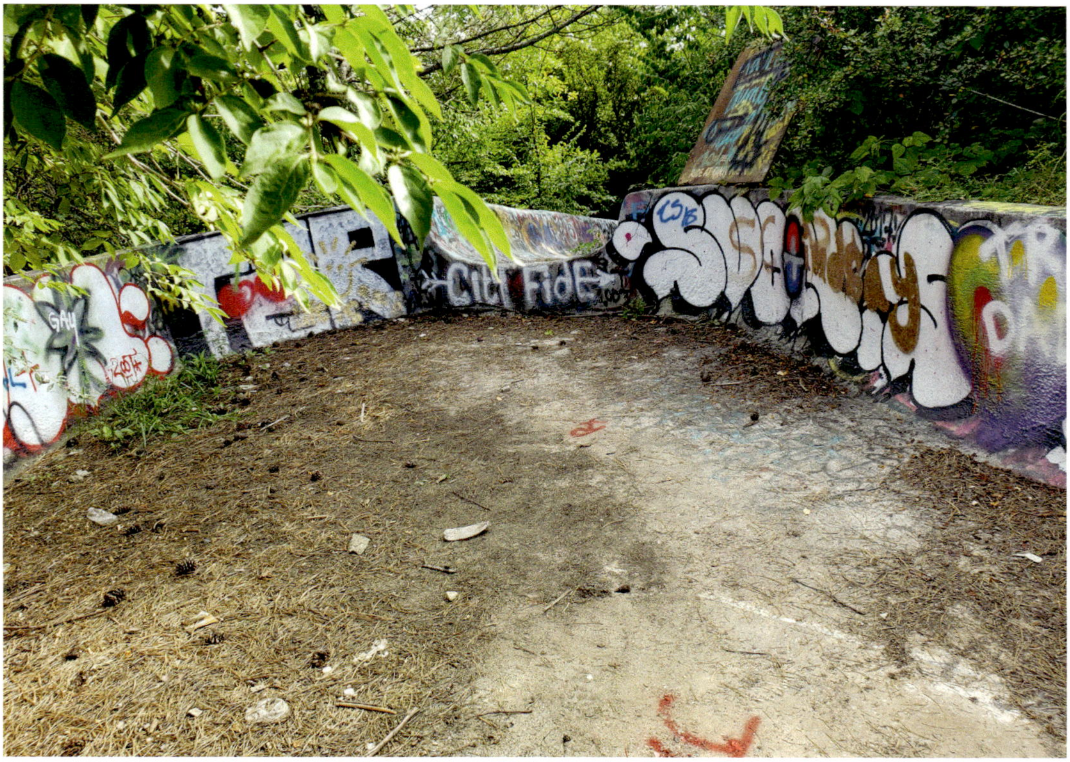

Slide origin pool, which was one of the only pools to not have standing water in it.

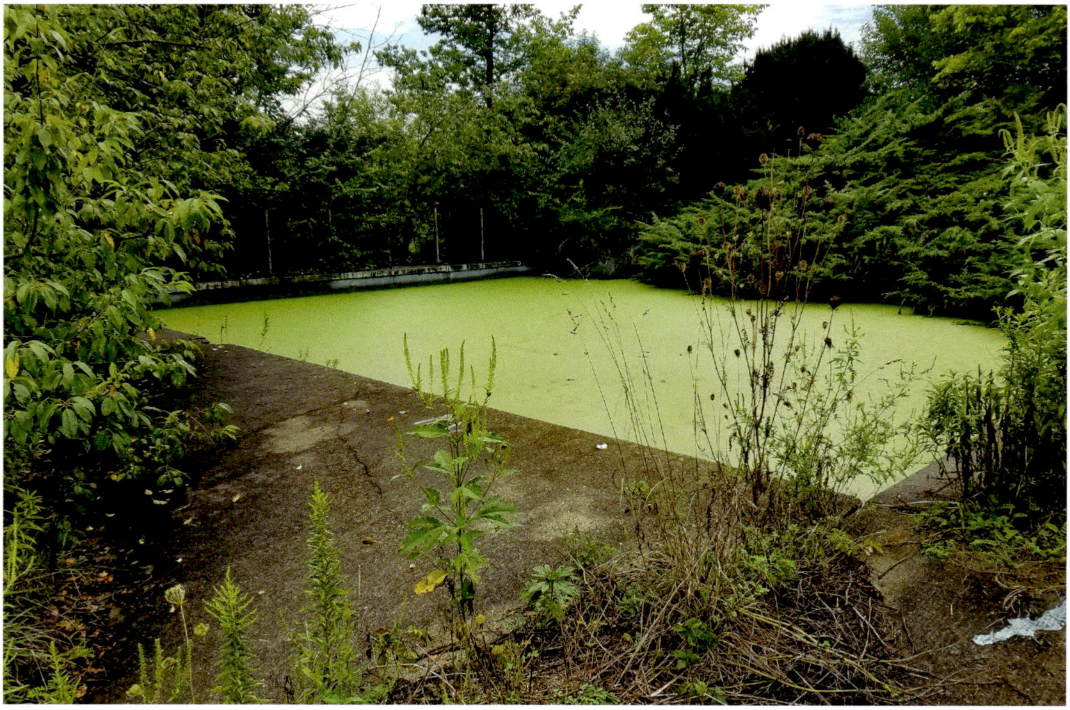

This pool was completely overgrown with thick, unpleasant smelling algae.

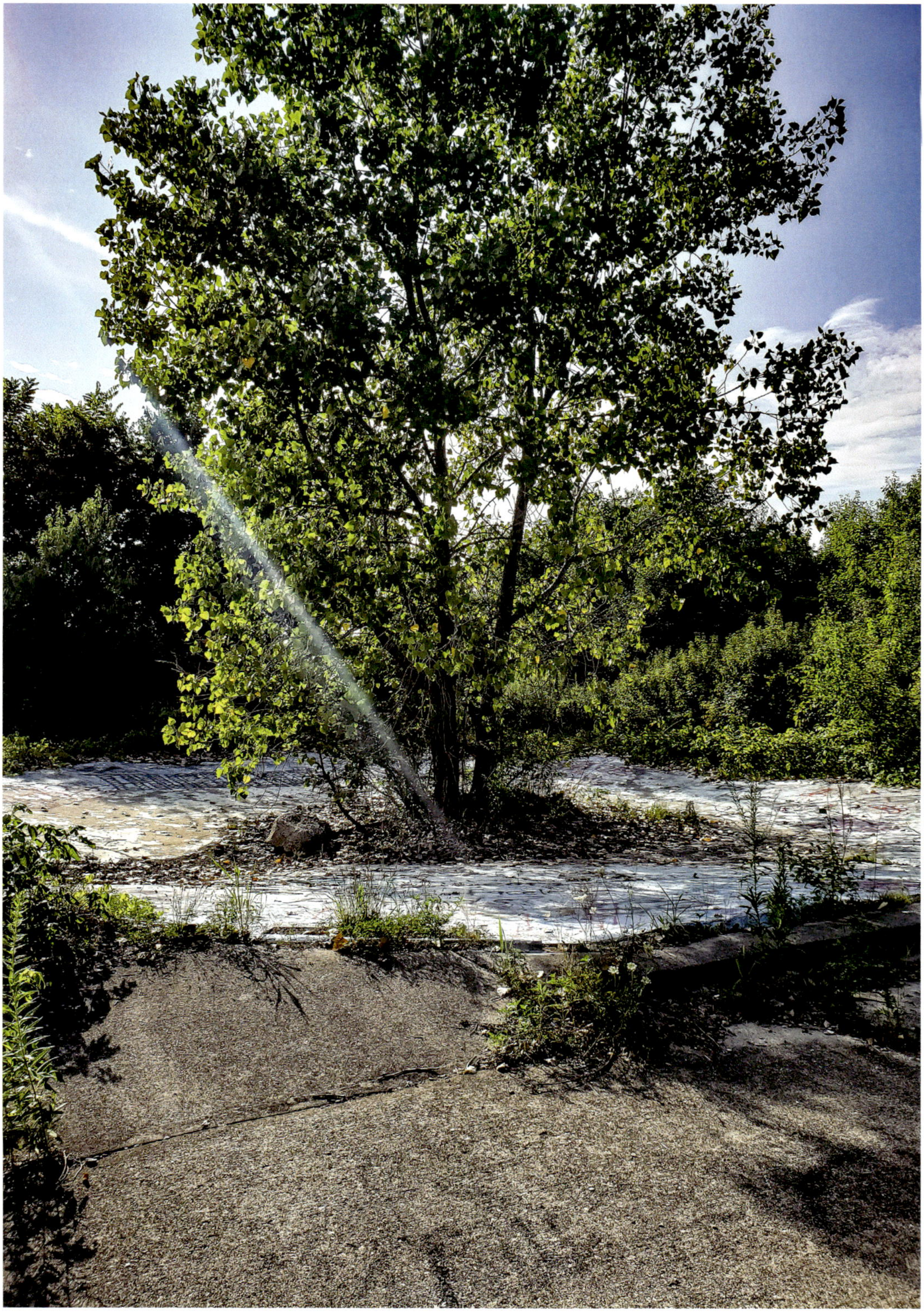

Over the years, nature had started reclaiming the park, which is how a tree began to grow in the middle of a kids' splash pool.

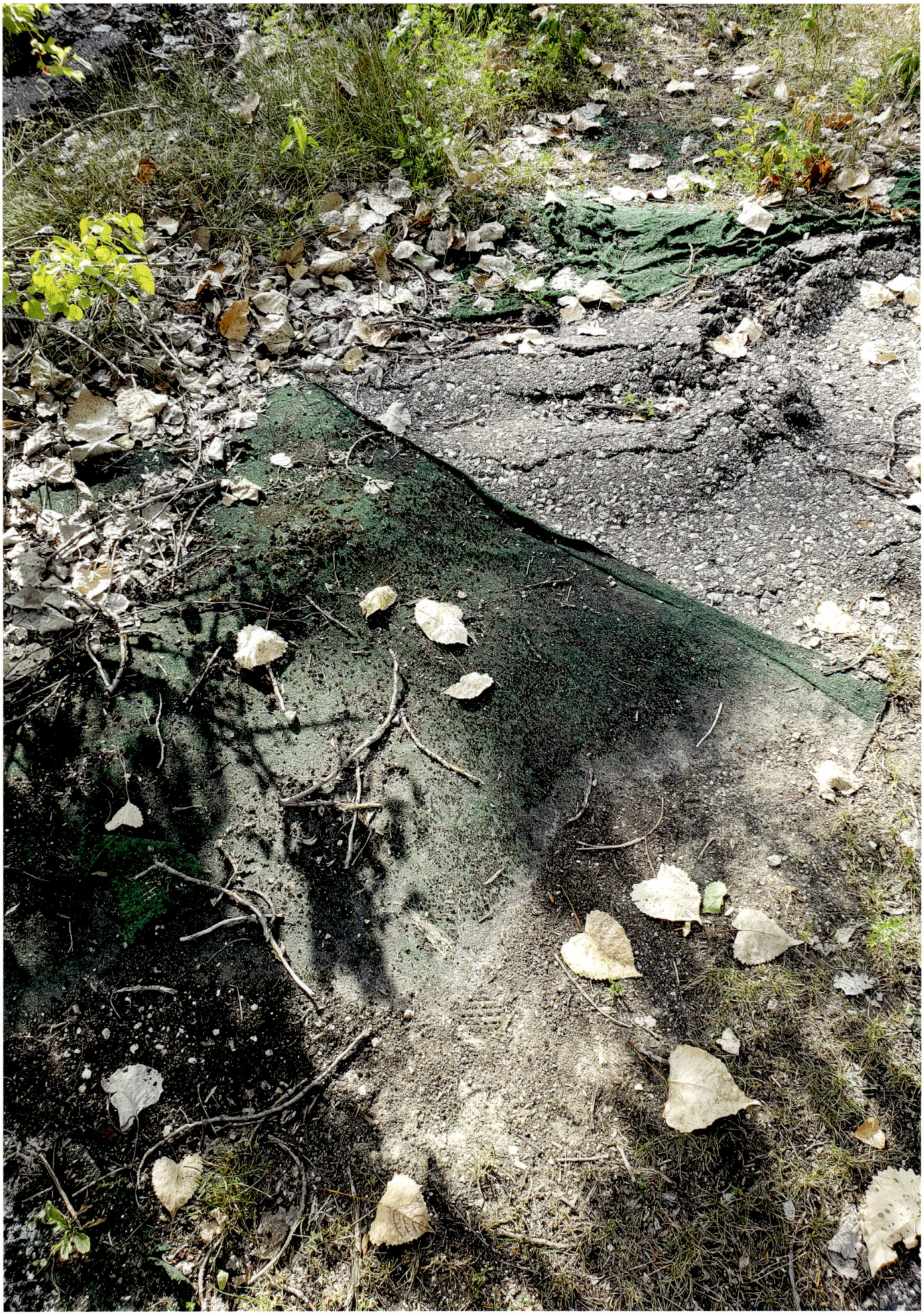

Under a lot of debris were the remains of the putt-putt course.

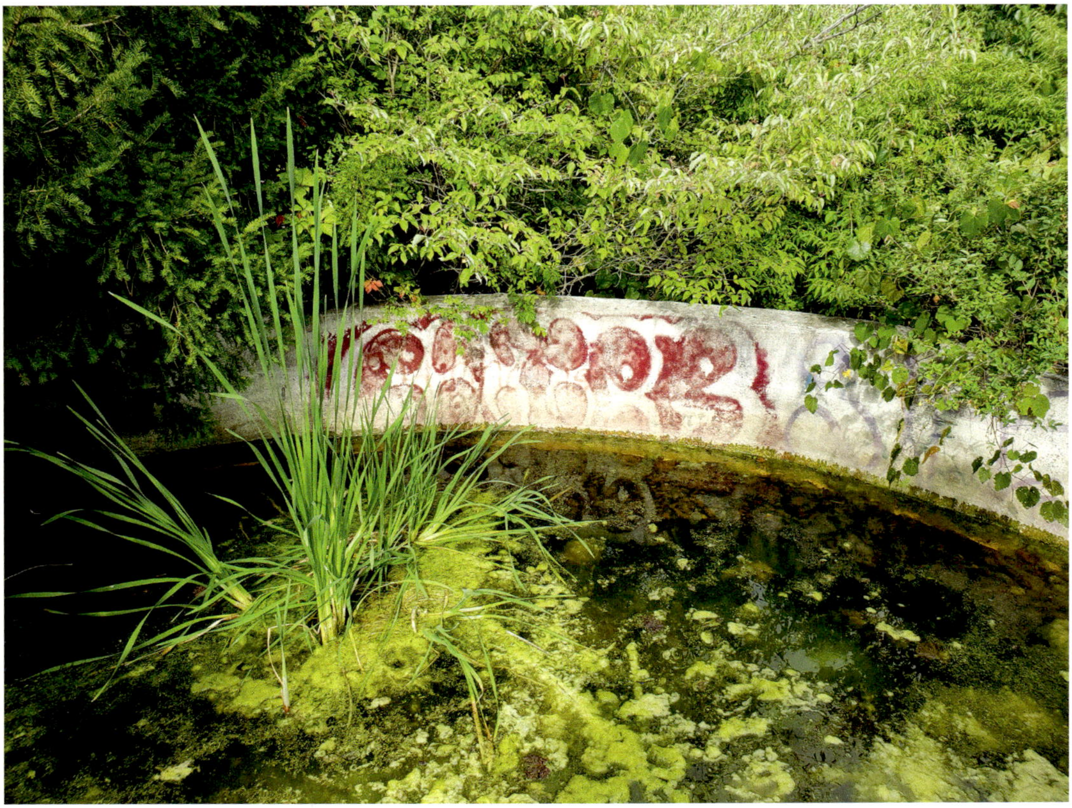

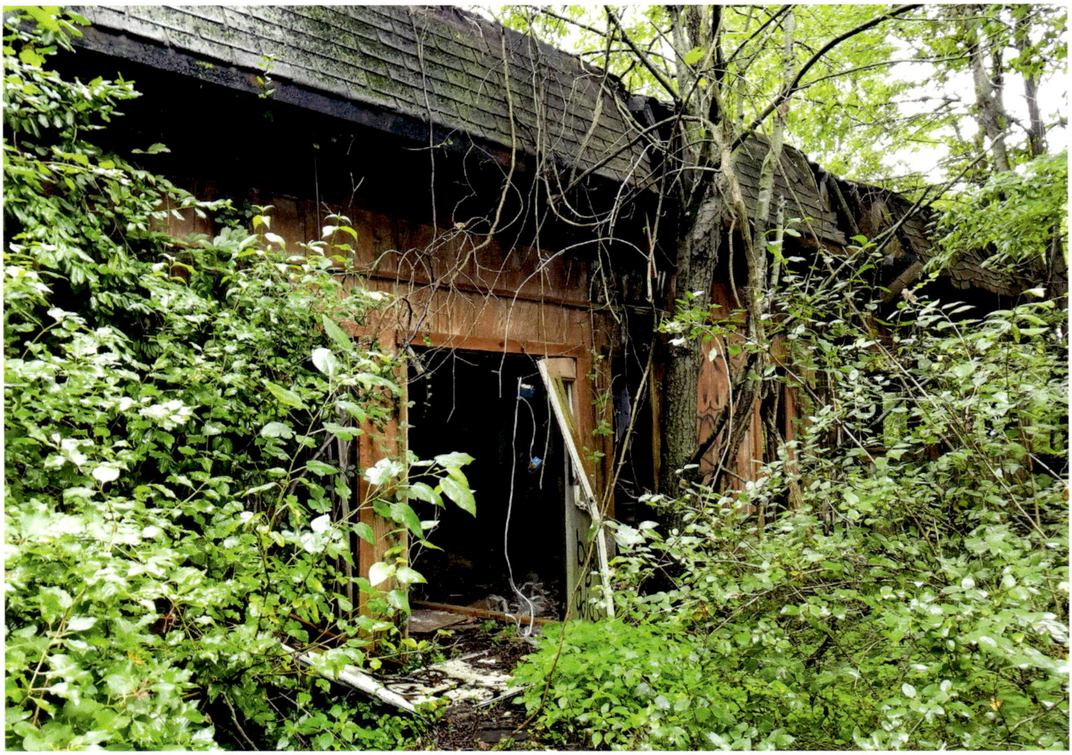

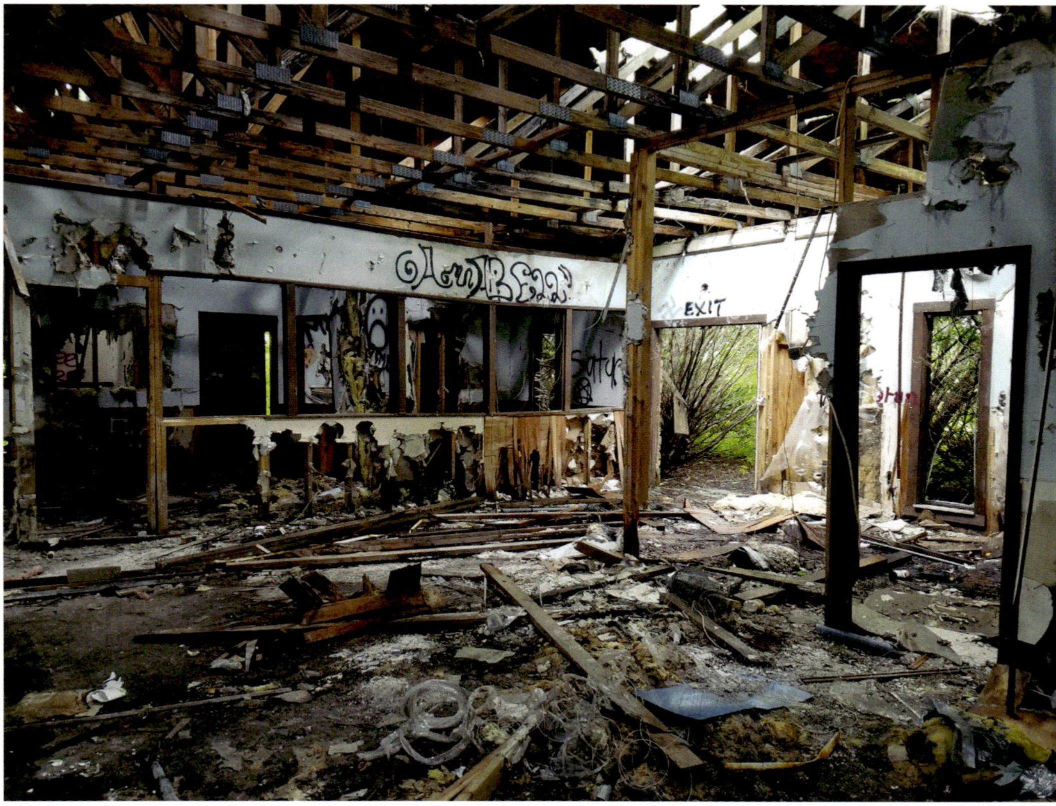

The inside of the clubhouse as photographed in 2018. When we did a second exploration in 2019, this building was completely gone.

Opposite above: A smaller pool that has become home to an entire ecosystem over the years.

Opposite below: Outside of the clubhouse, which at one point had caught on fire.

6

REMNANTS

Side-of-the-road finds have always been my absolute favorite, driving through the country and suddenly spotting a beautiful house in the middle of a crop of trees, or a restaurant on the side of the road, or even a small-town school that closed because of consolidation. Finding locations that look like they were just suddenly left overnight is one of the best feelings—it's like walking straight into the past.

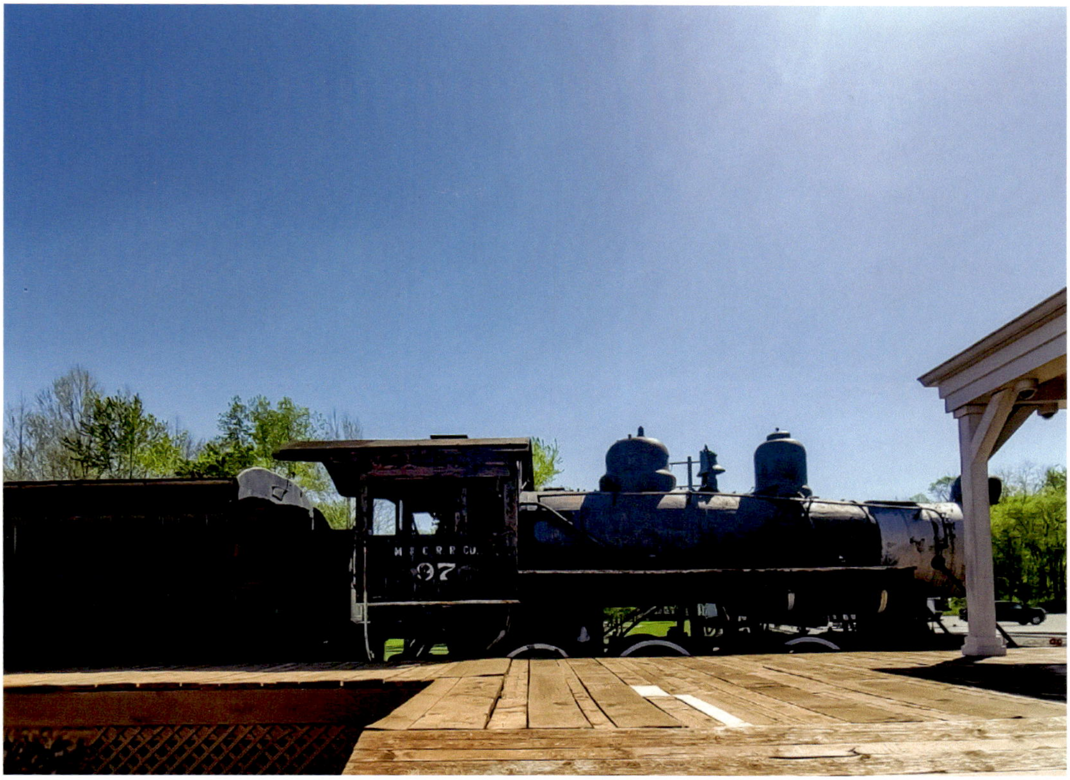

Above: We got a tip about an abandoned train/mail car from a fellow explorer.

Right: Front of the train by what was once a transportation museum that closed during the pandemic.

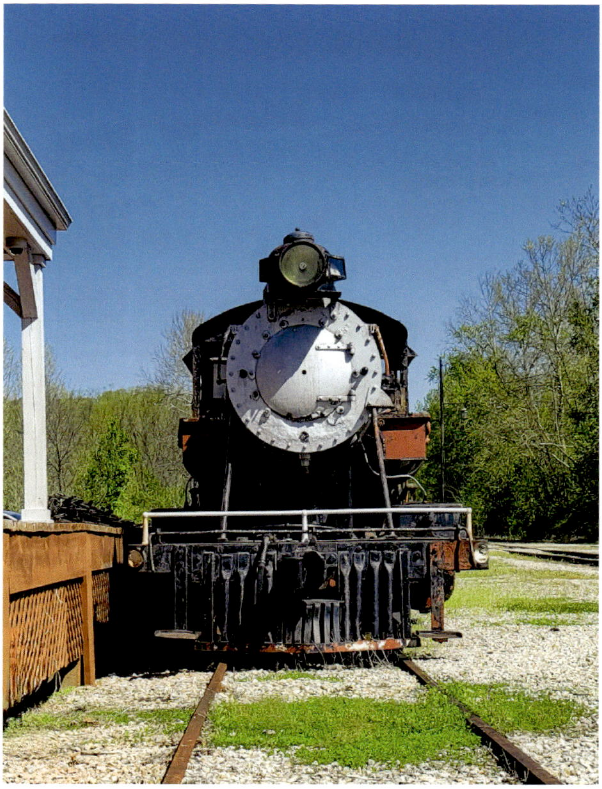

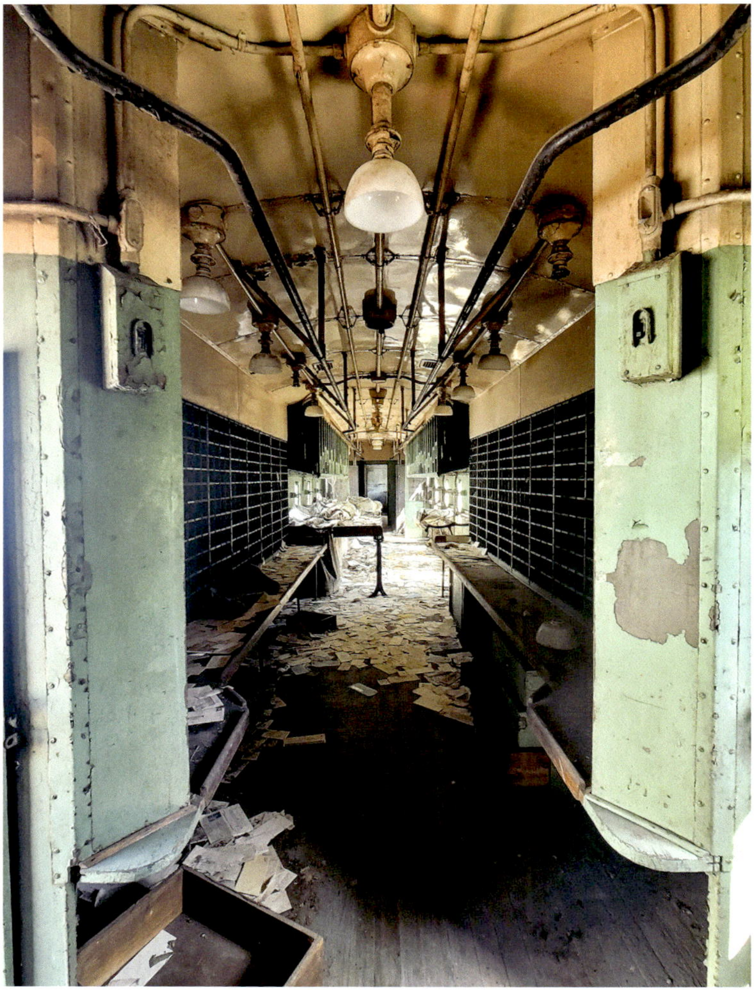

Left: The view when you first step into the mail car.

Below: Many of the compartments were left open, and there is mail littering the floor.

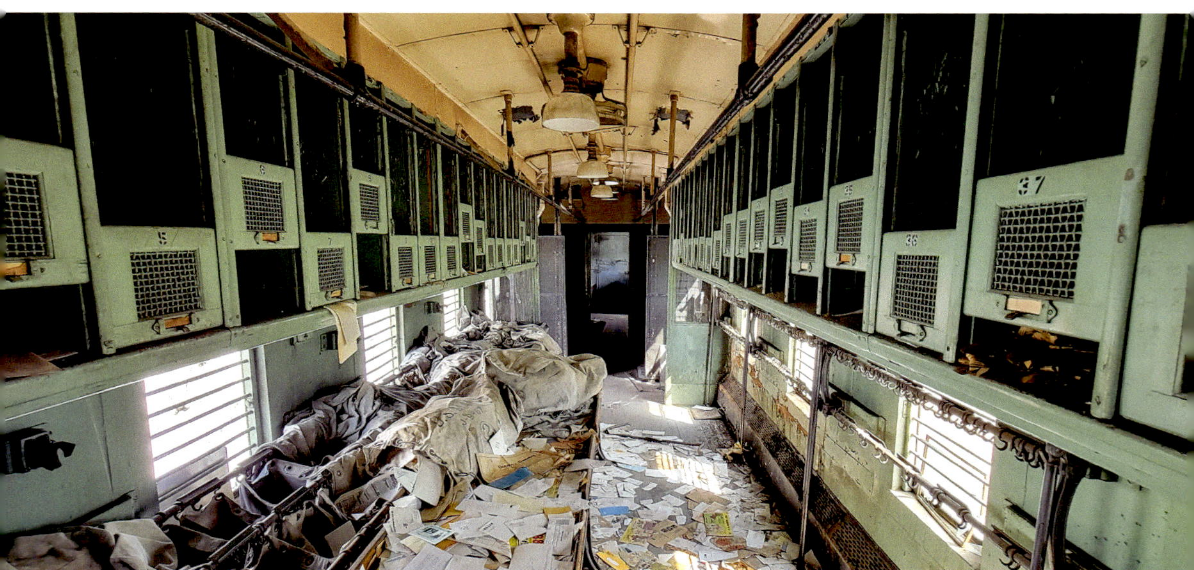

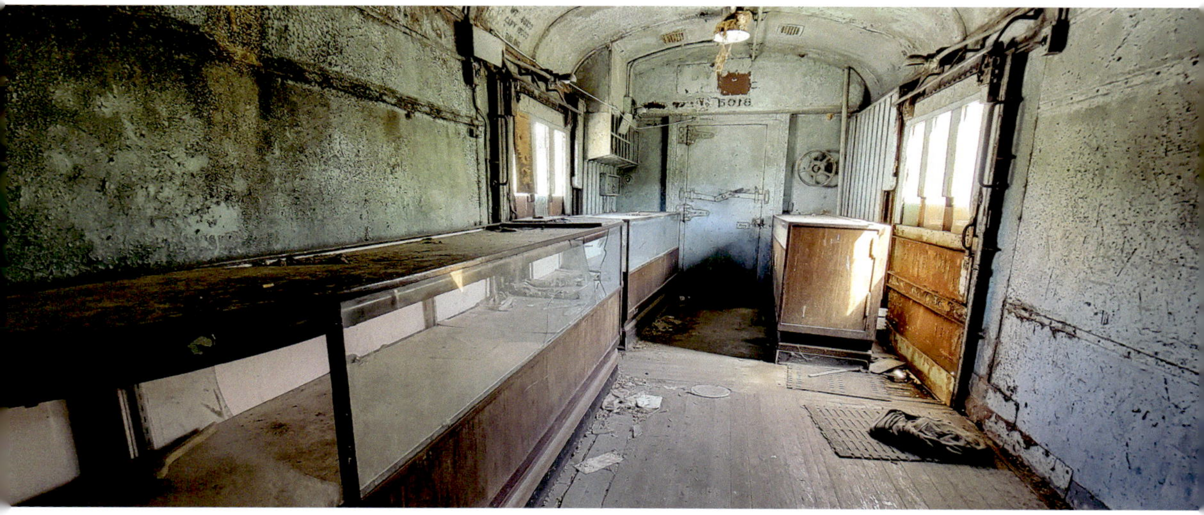

The shop car. I assume at one point you could purchase mailing supplies here.

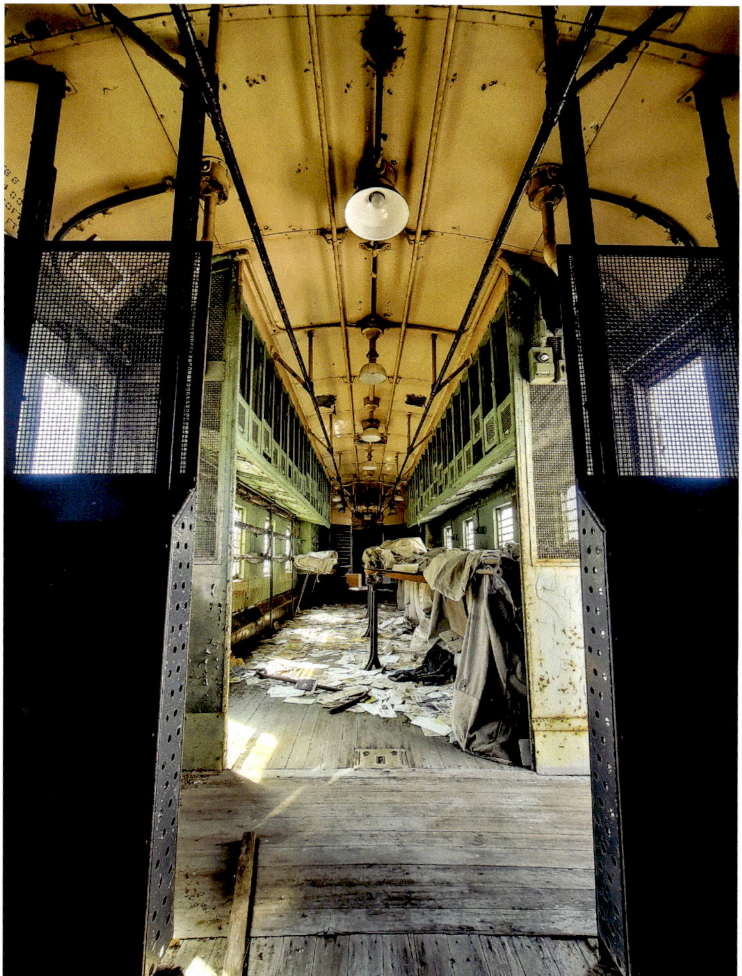

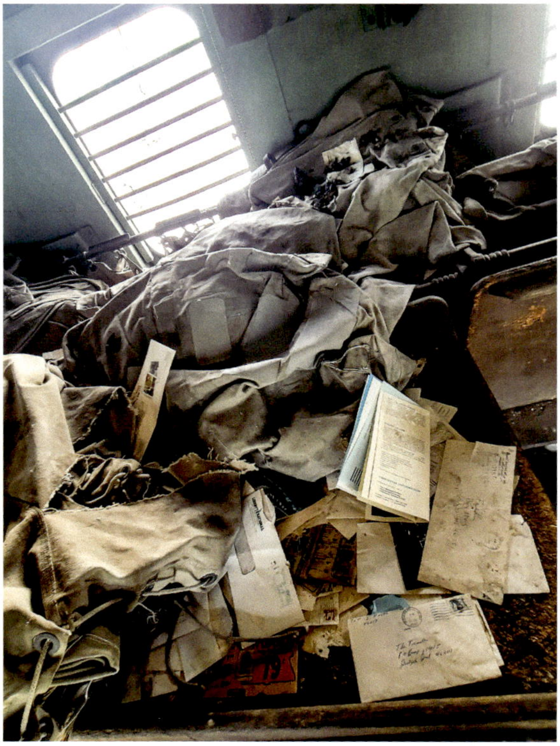

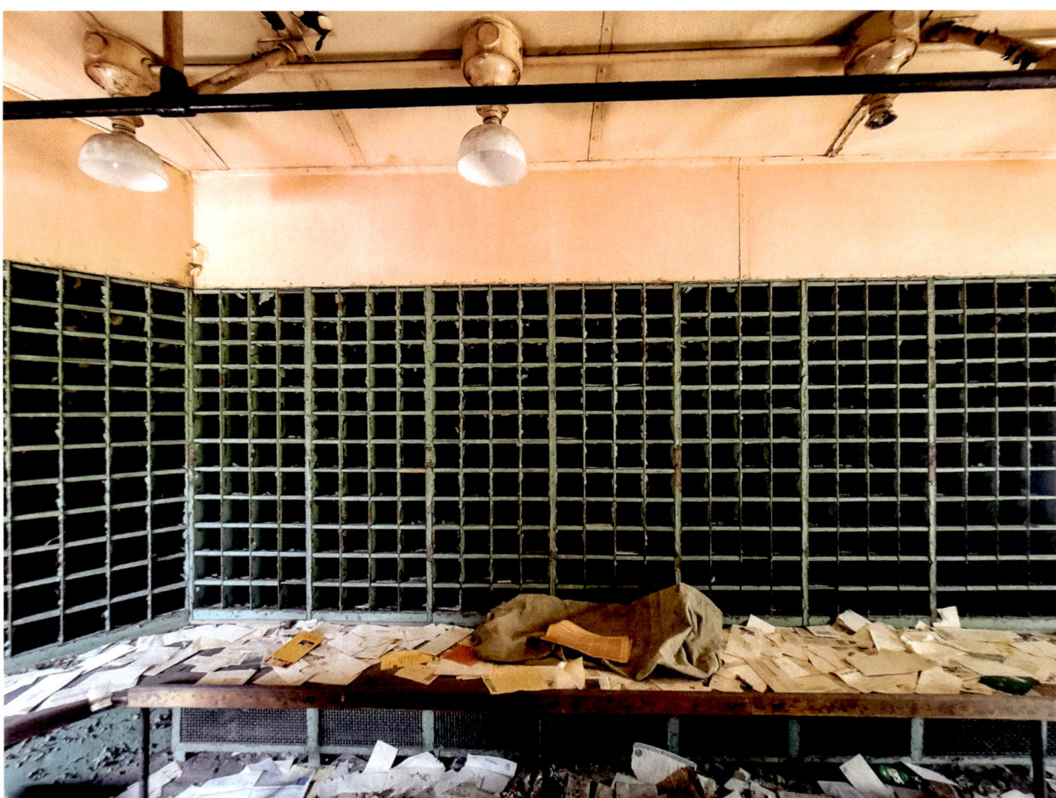

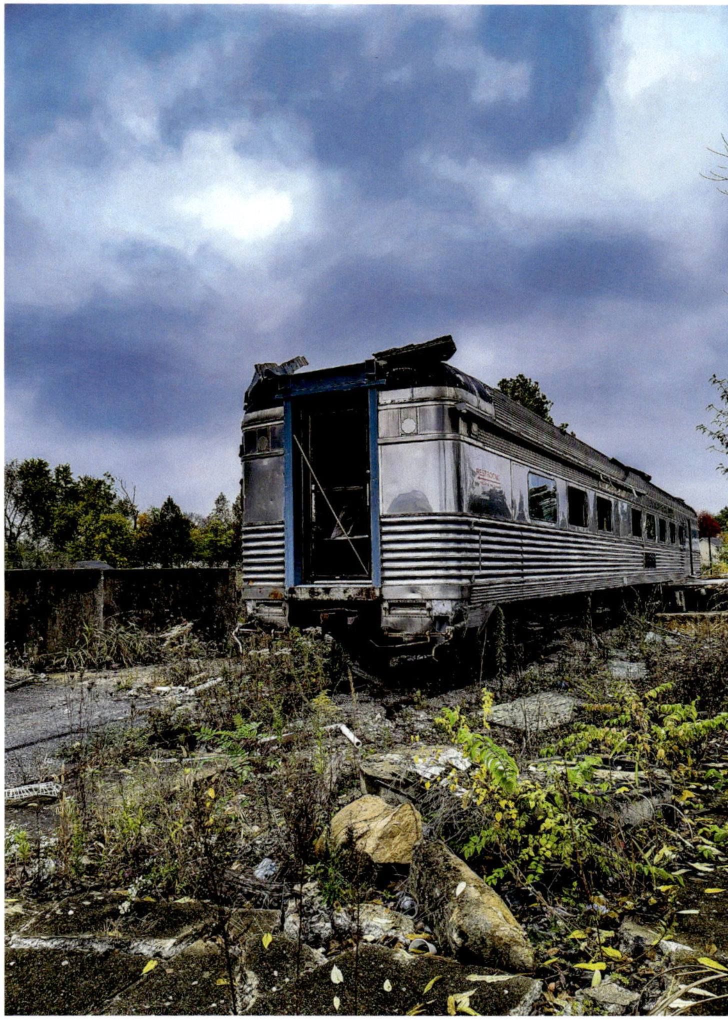

Right: We had gone this direction for a specific location (which was a bust), but found this on the side of the road.

Below: When we peeked inside, we realized it was a former restaurant, with the booths still left inside.

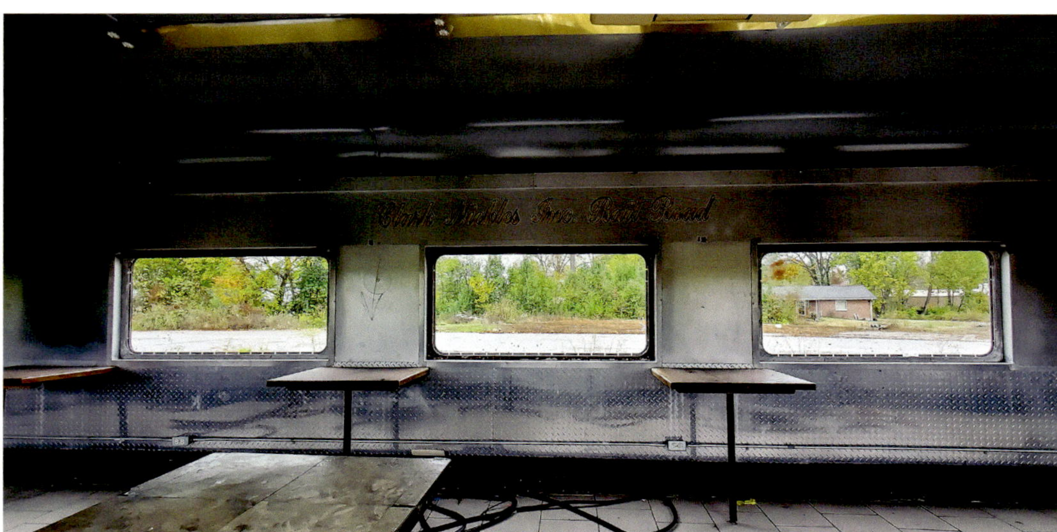

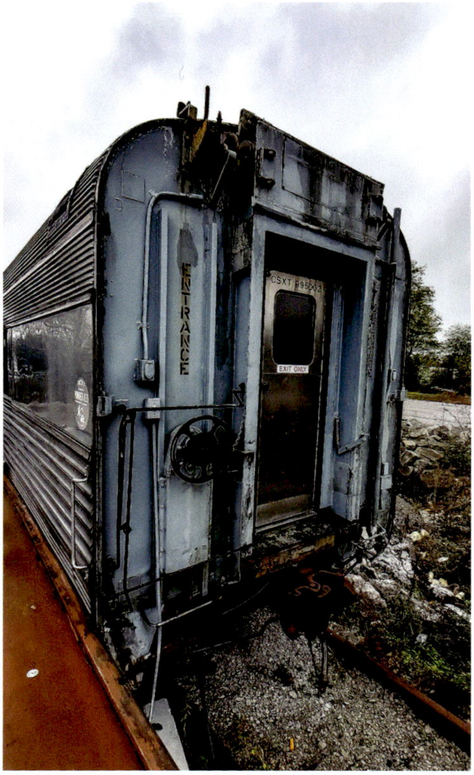

Left: This door was either rusted shut or locked; either way, we couldn't open it.

Below: Side view with the name "Clark Nickels Inc. Rail Road" visible.

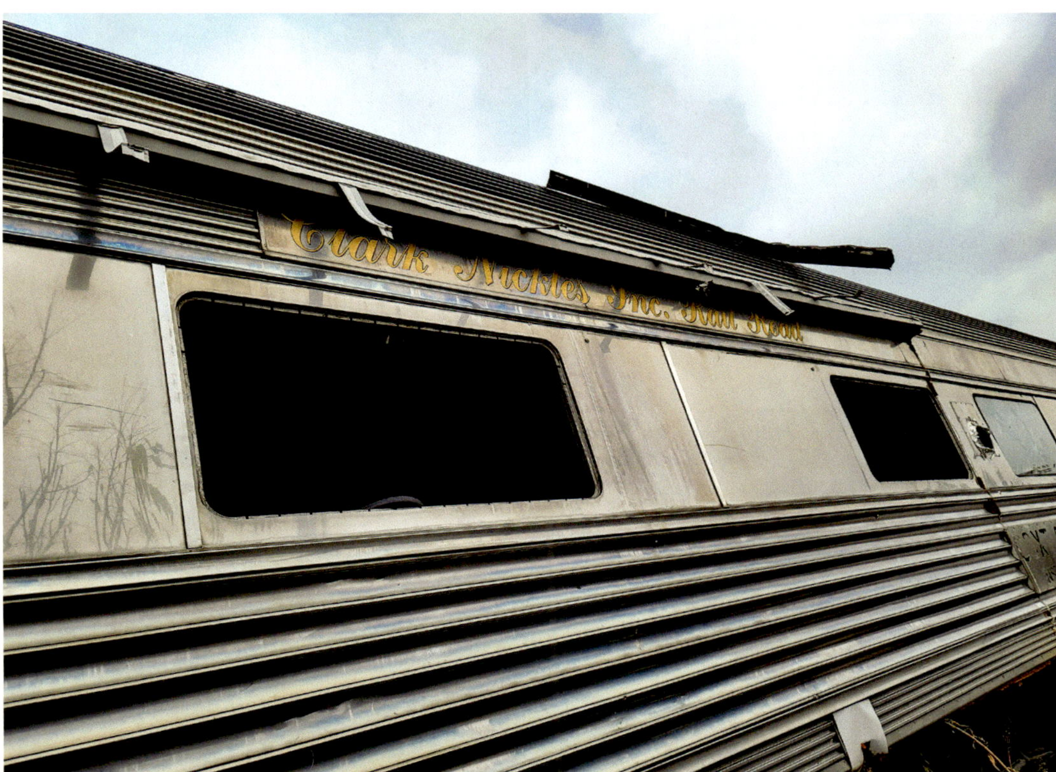

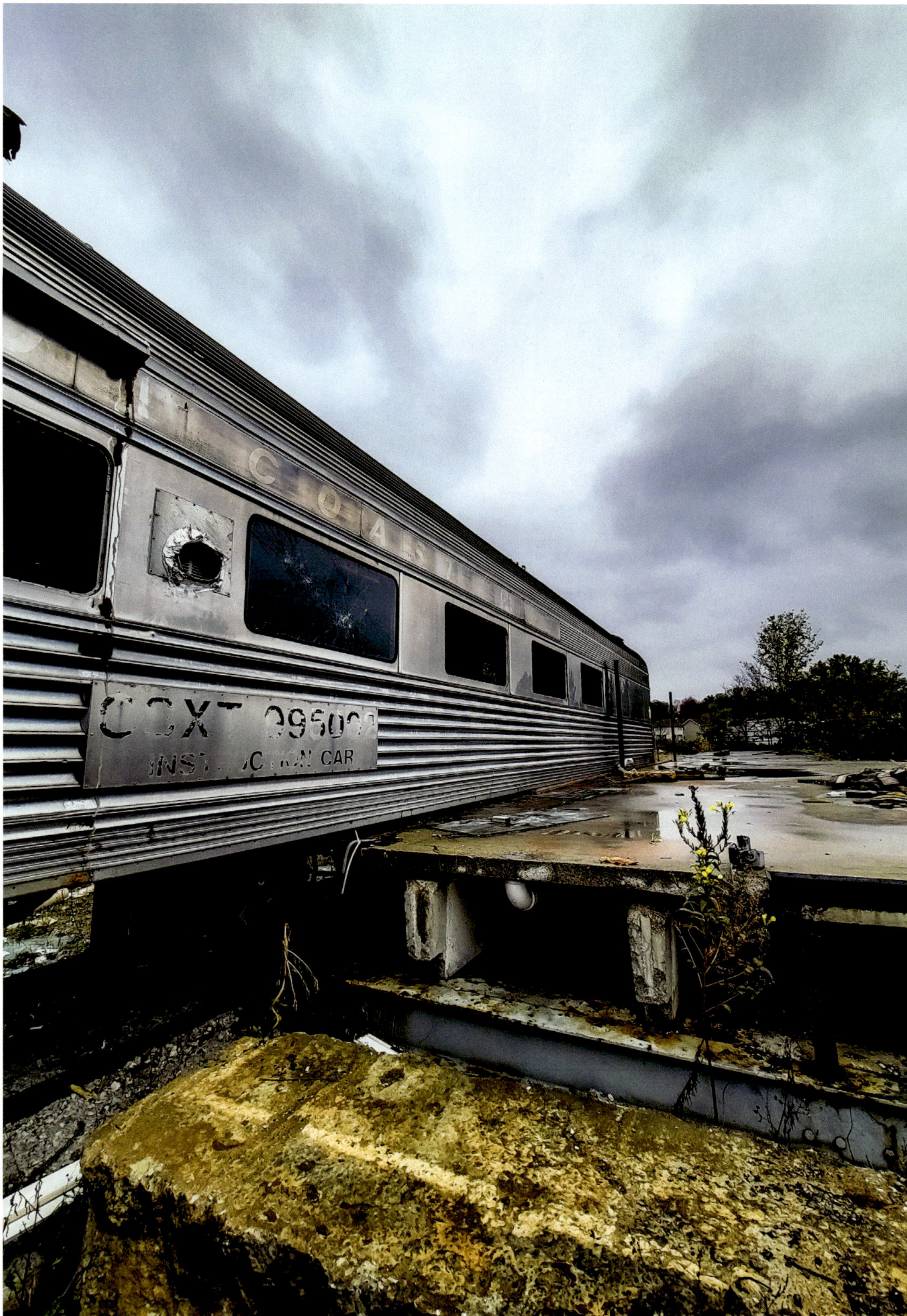

The stairs and landing, which is how it is assumed patrons would enter the restaurant.

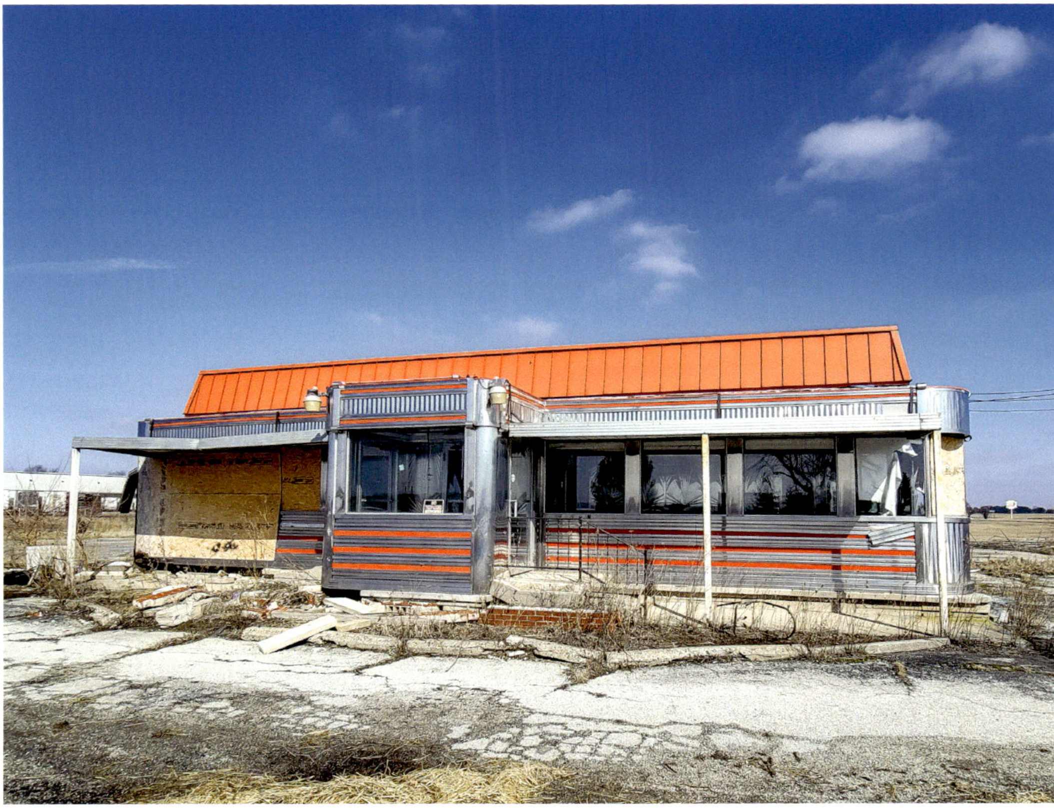

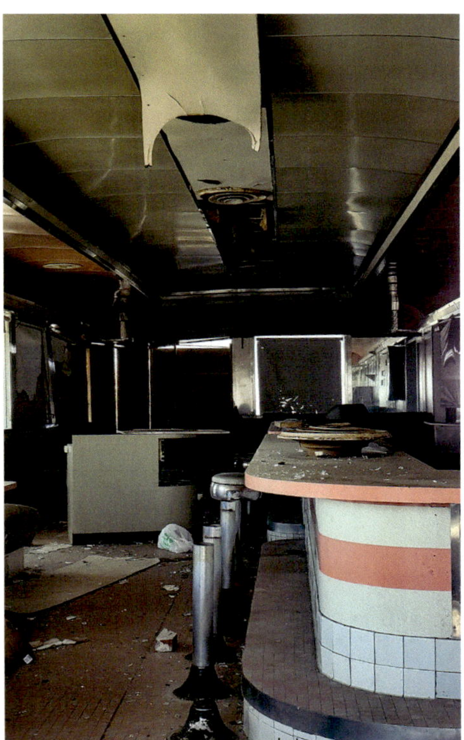

Above: We passed this diner all the time on our way to concerts, and we finally made time to stop by.

Left: The front counter. The left side of the diner was crashed into by a car shortly before it was photographed.

Right: Main booths next to the window, facing US-52.

Below: Eventually the diner was purchased by someone who has plans to renovate it after moving it to a new location.

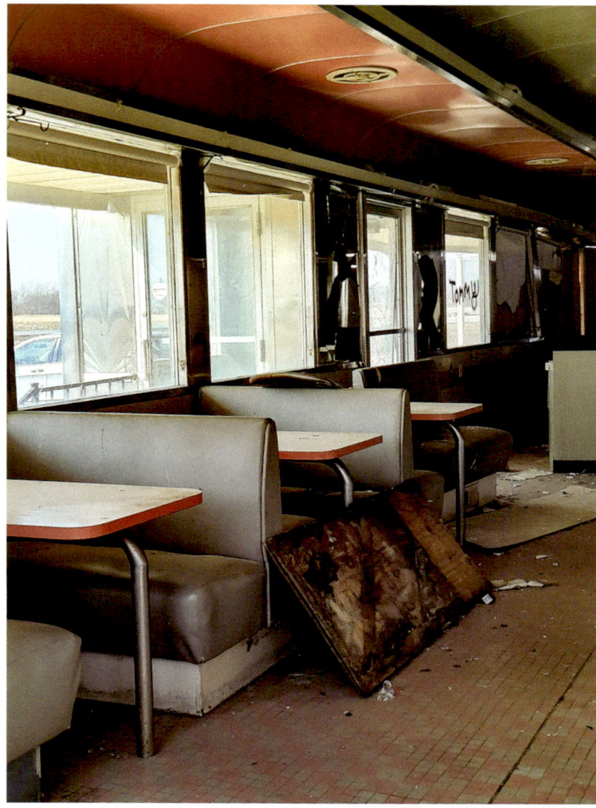

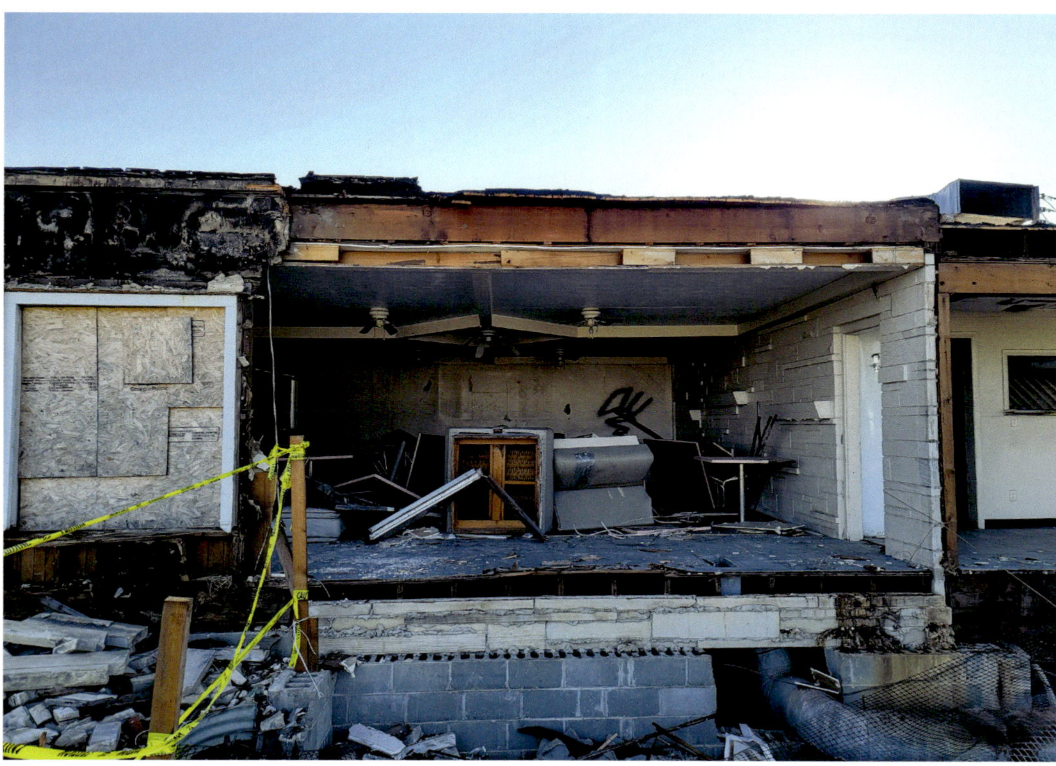

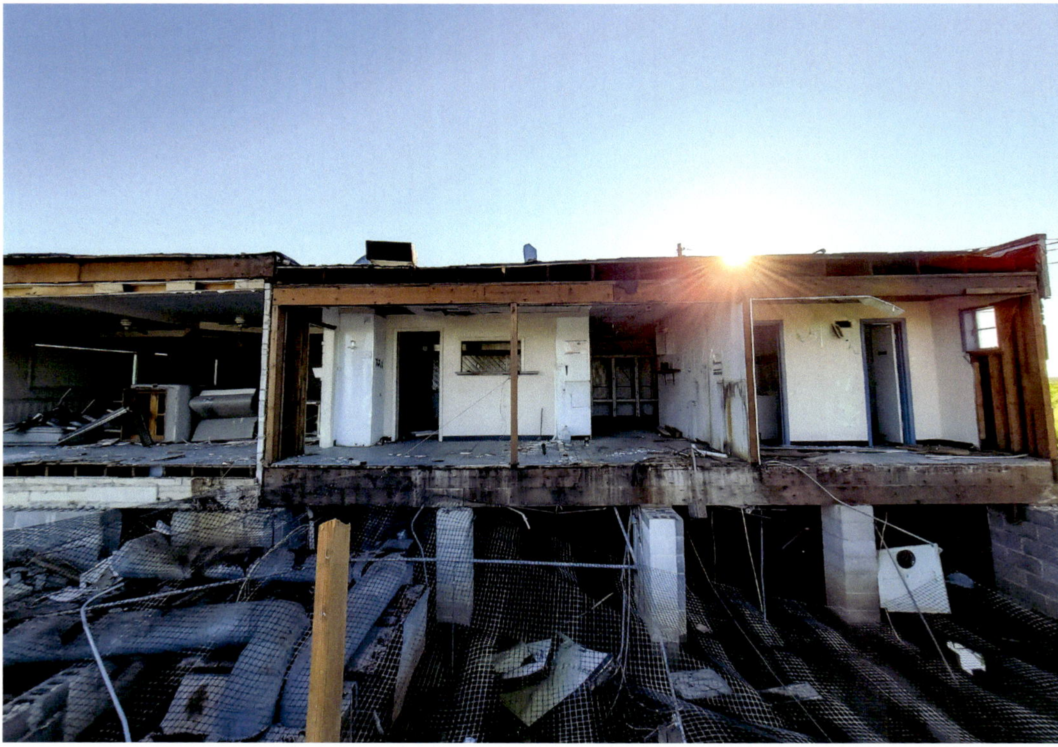

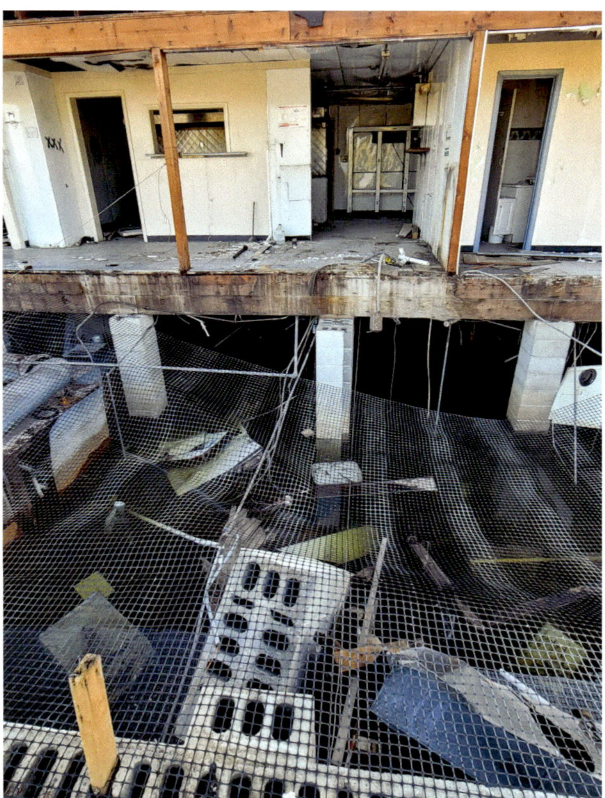

Above: They moved it in pieces; while the front had already been relocated, the back had not.

Left: The underside of the building was interesting to see.

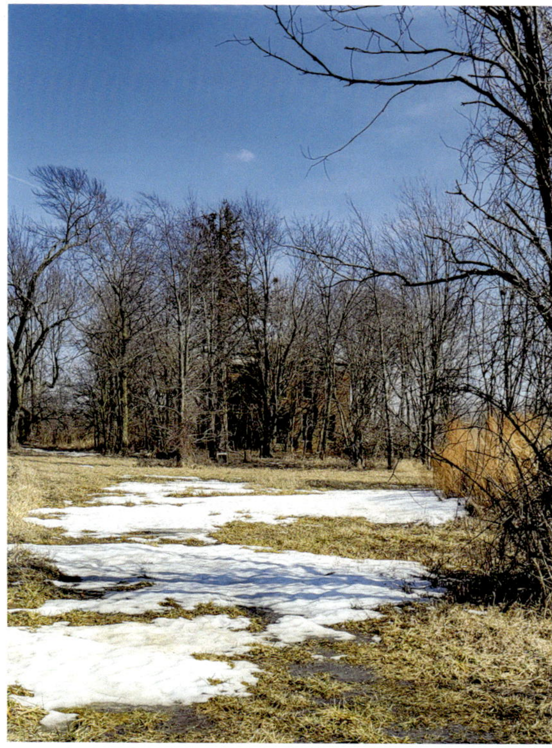

Right: We spotted this house nestled in the middle of some trees on our way home from a concert one day, so we marked it on the map to return.

Below: I really liked the star accents on the outside of the house.

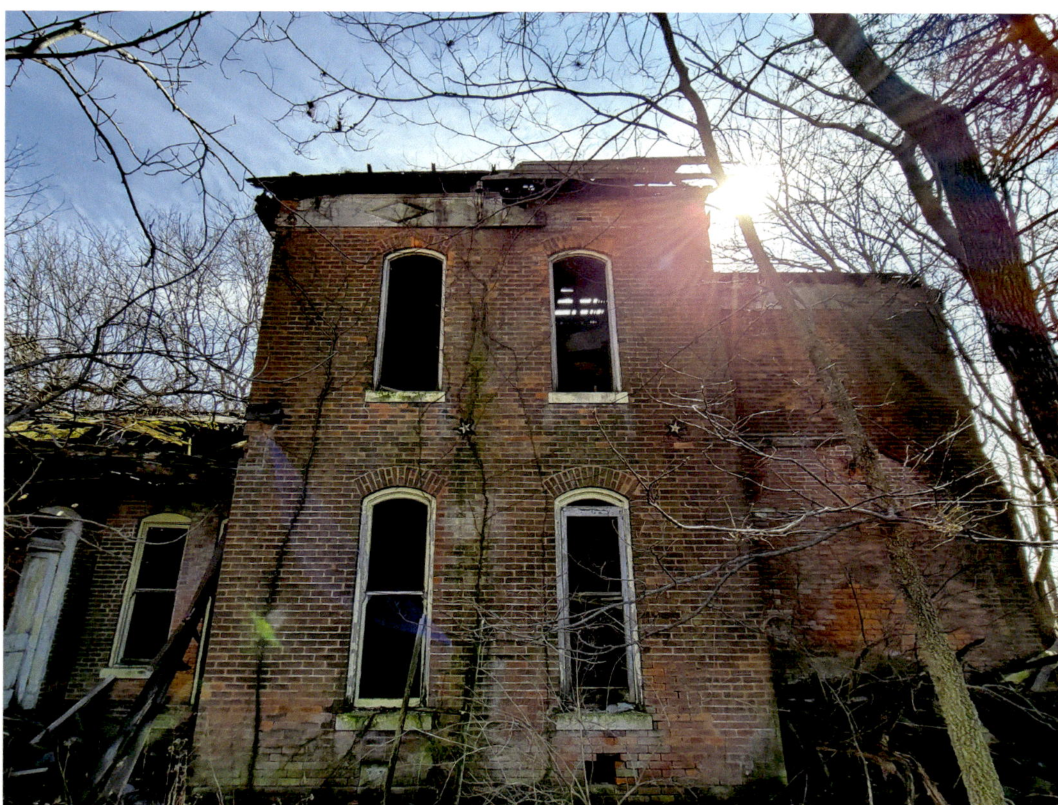

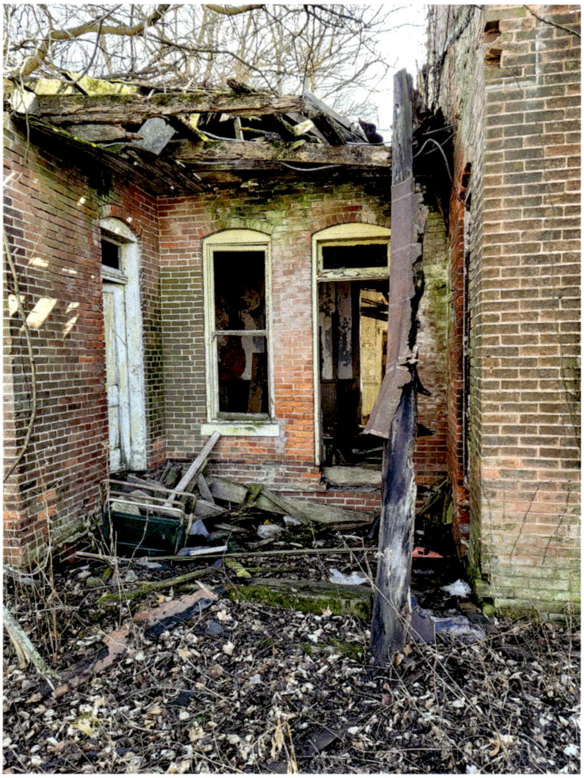

The side entrance to the house.

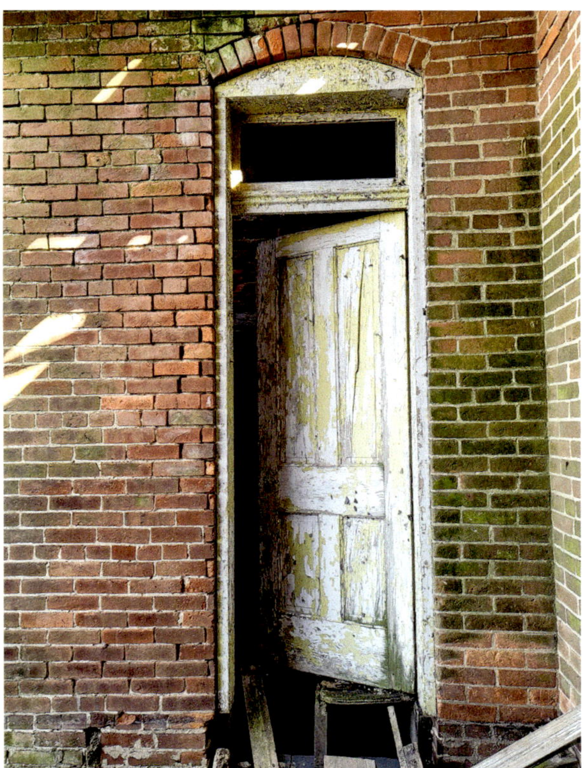

A door left slightly open. The floor underneath is gone.

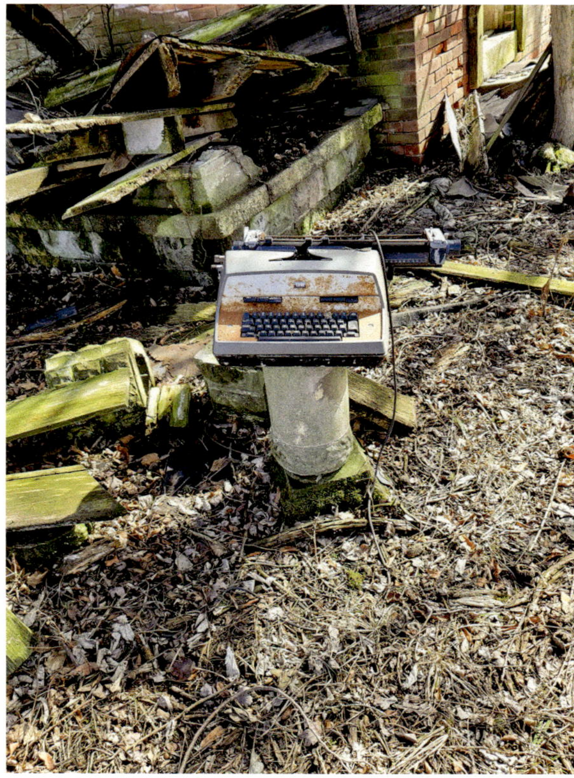

An old typewriter set up on pieces of concrete.

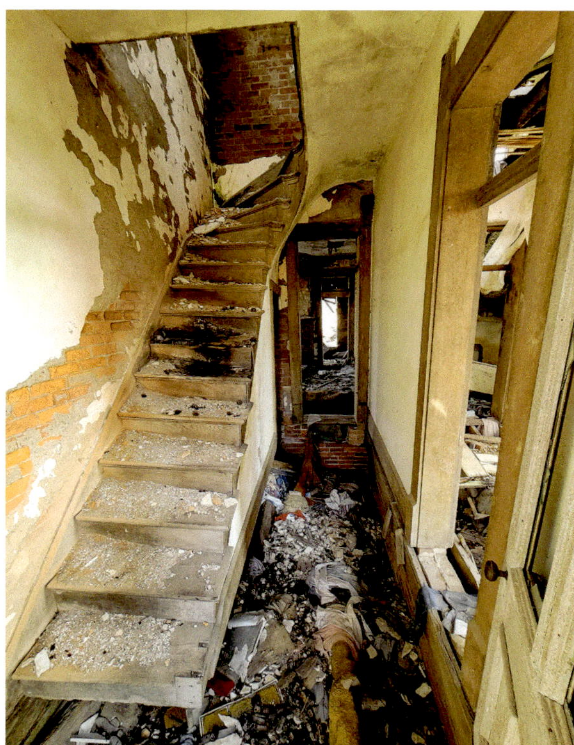

The view from the front entrance. The stairs no longer reach the floor since the floor has rotted away.

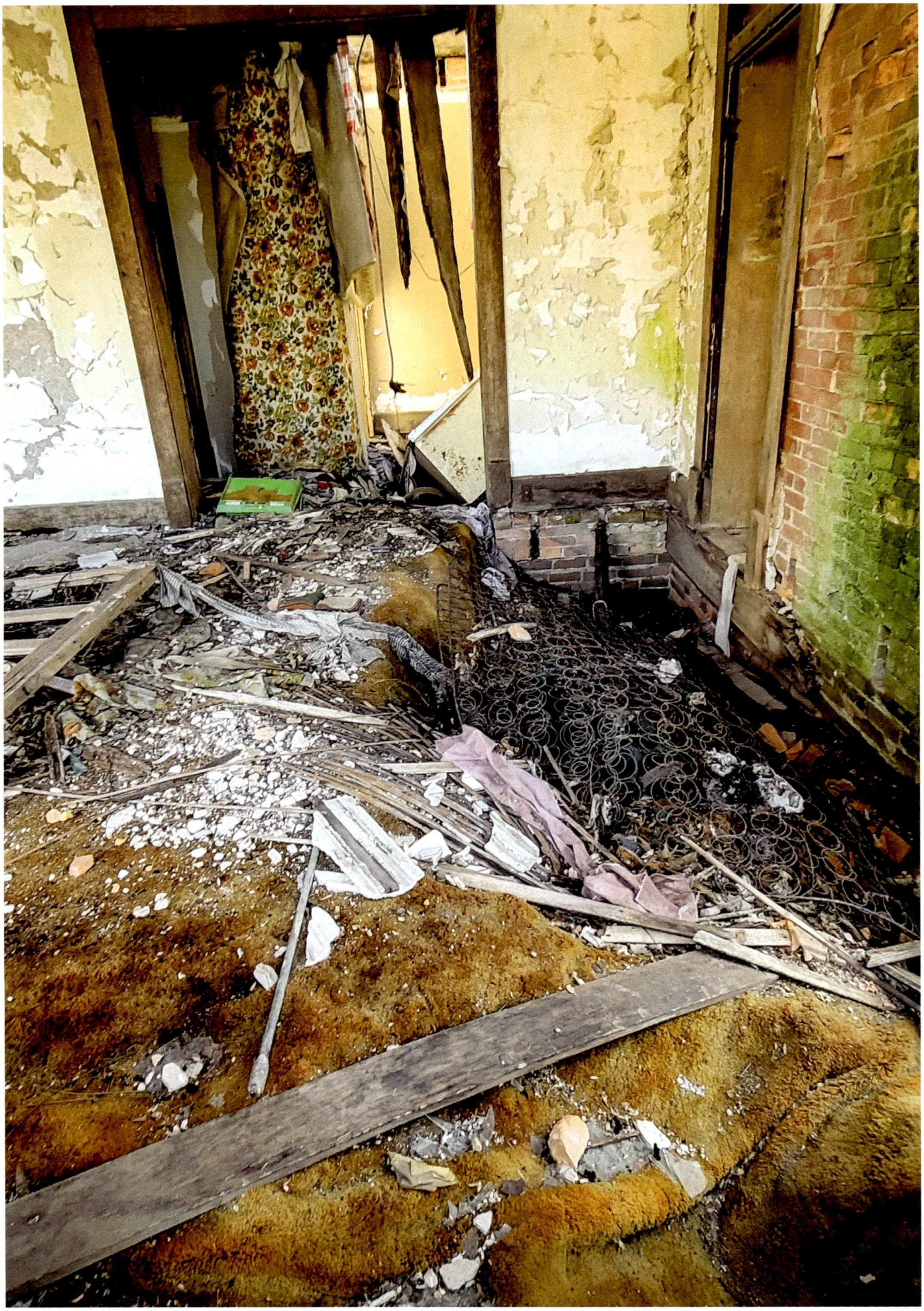

What I assume had been the living room. There are springs left on the ground. I'm unsure if they're from an old couch or bed.

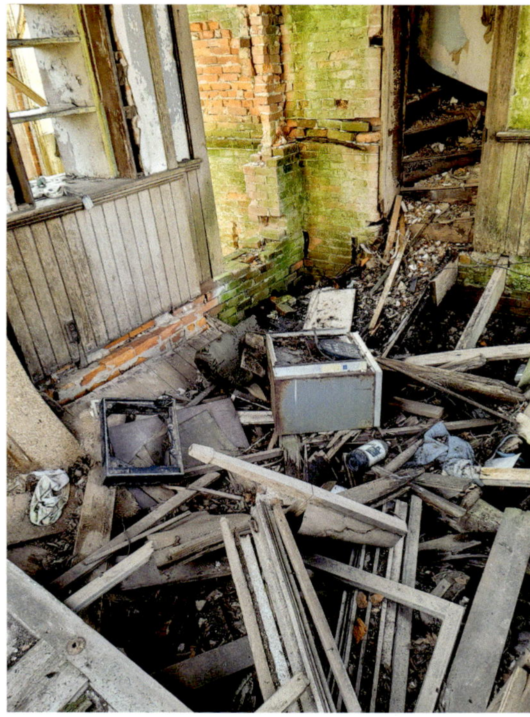

The backside of the house had this tiny room and a small set of stairs, which were originally most likely used by servants.

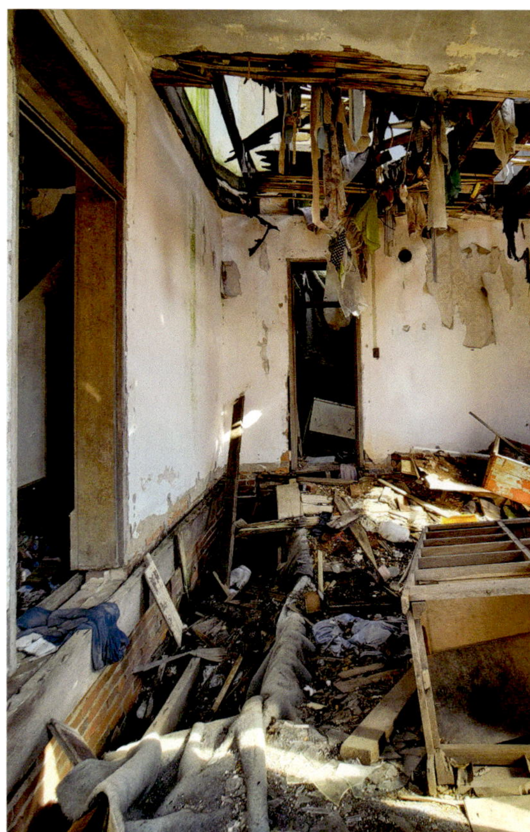

The front room also had a ceiling that was collapsing. It looked like the room above was a bedroom judging from the clothing hanging down.

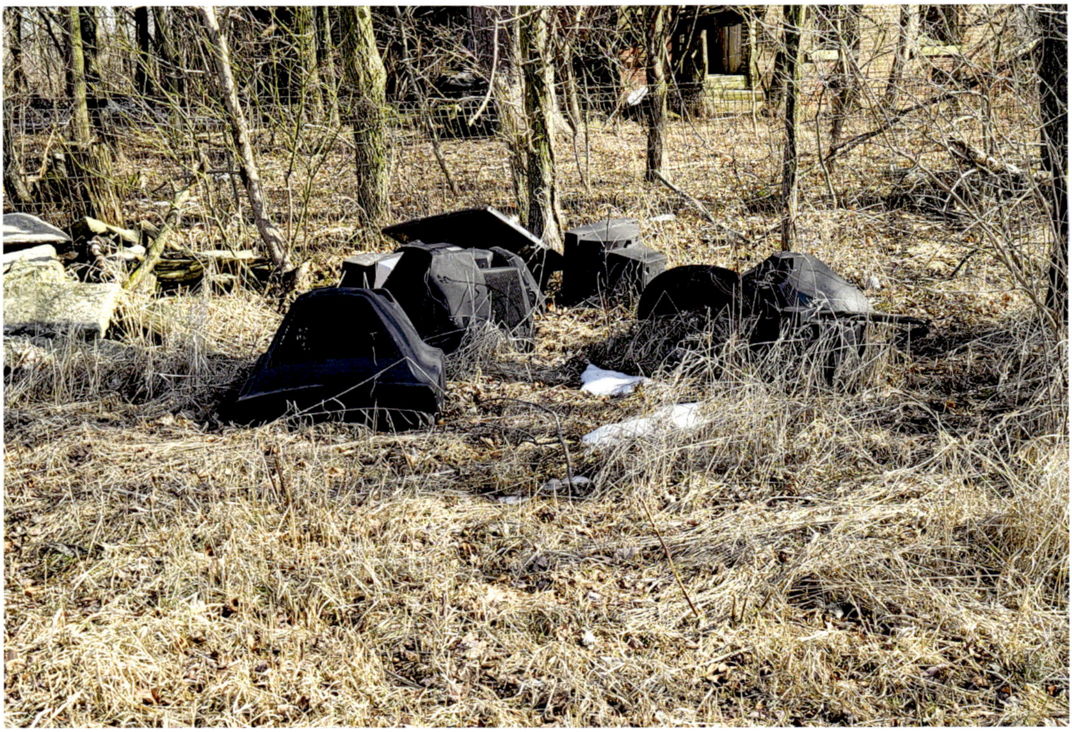

There were a surprising amount of TVs left in one specific area of the property.

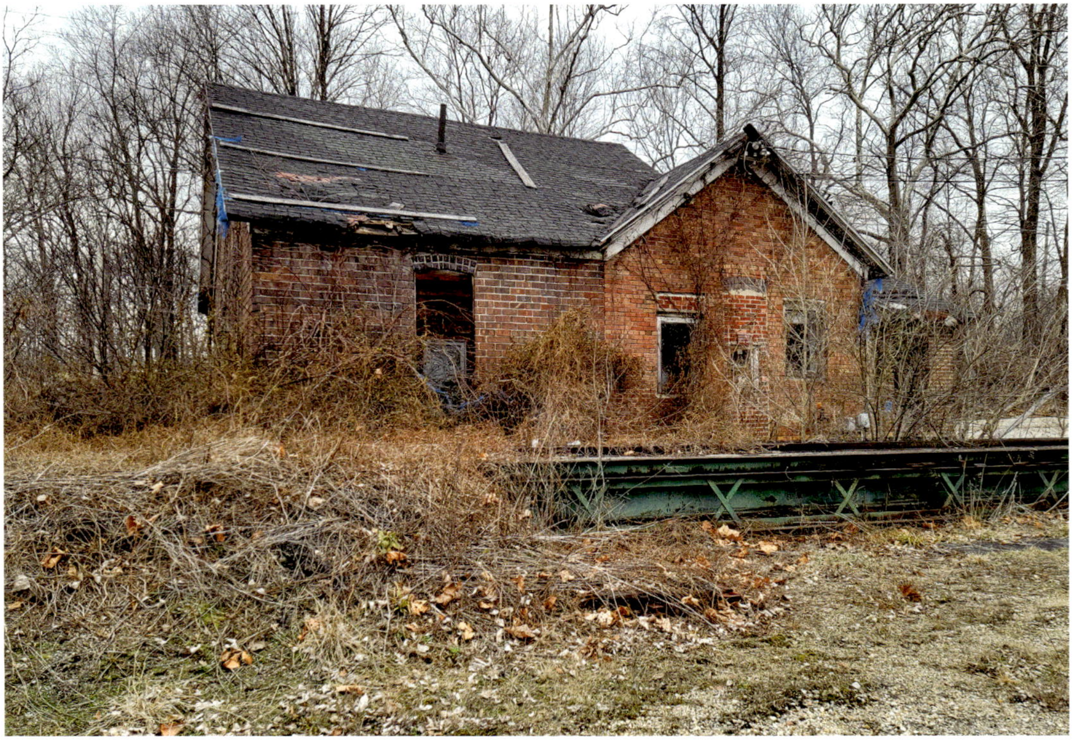

At one point, this was operated as a full junkyard.

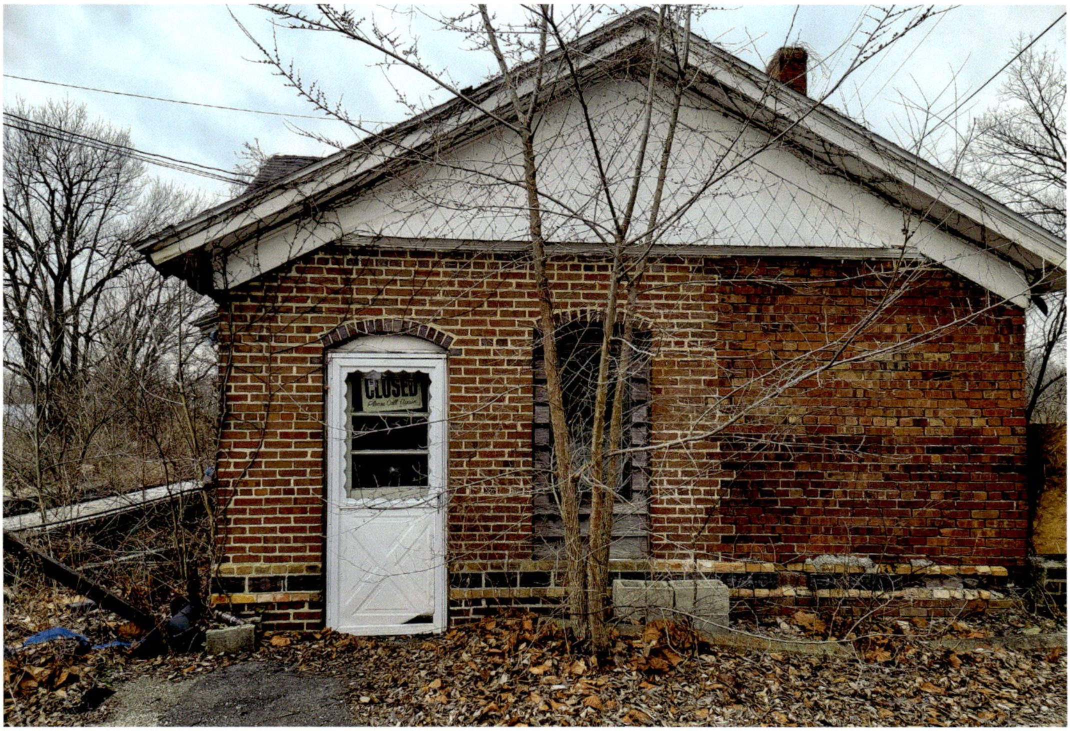

They decided to turn the house into an office. The closed sign is still on the door.

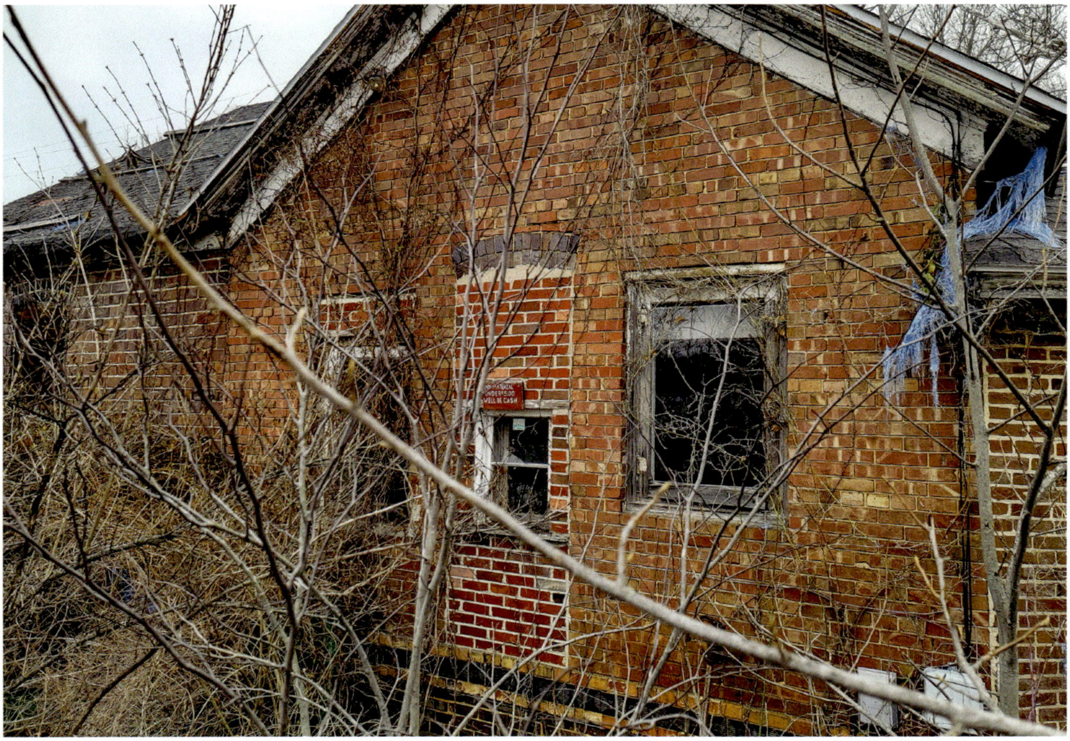

They added a drive-through window to the house/office. The sign states that "any material under 5.00 will be cash."

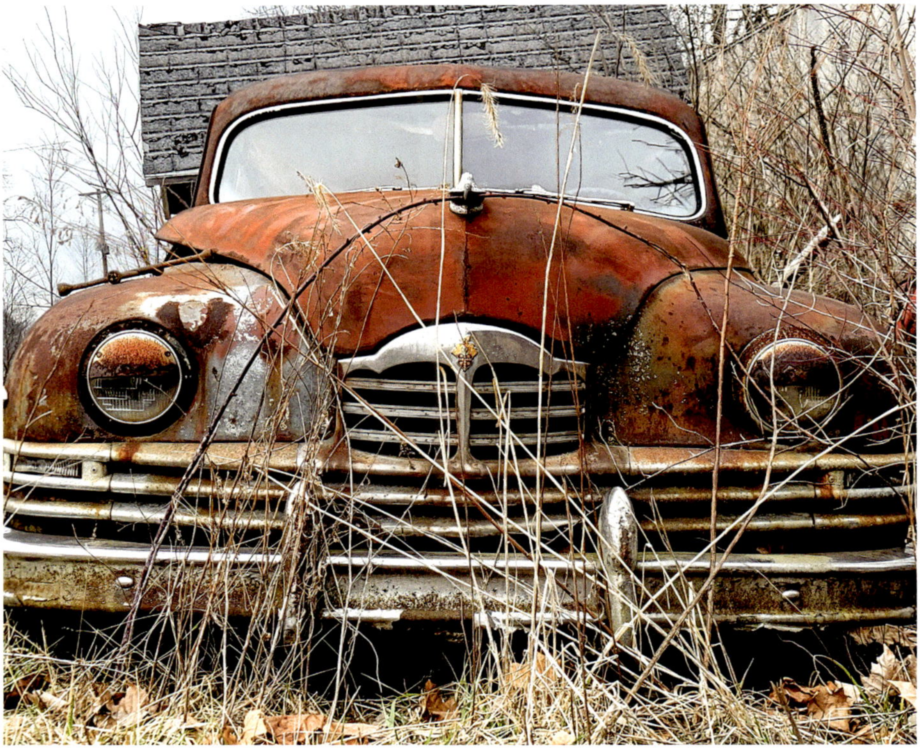

A 1949 Packard 22 Series Deluxe 8 touring sedan rusts away in the Indiana winter.

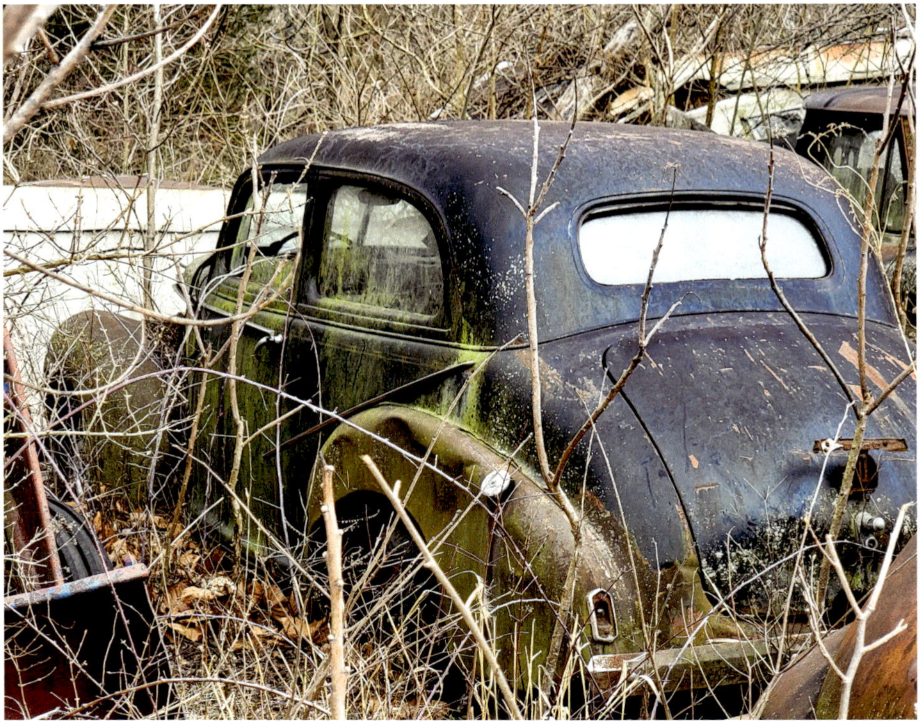

A 1940 Chevrolet Master Deluxe covered in moss.

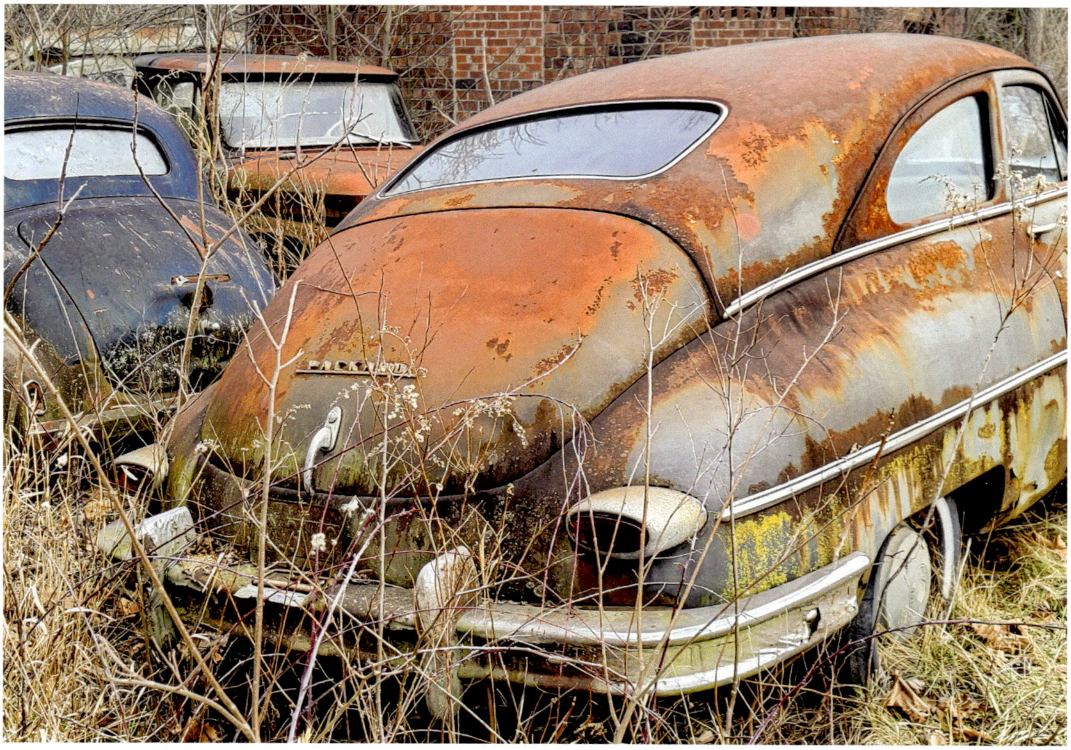

A second Packard Deluxe 8 has been left to decay.

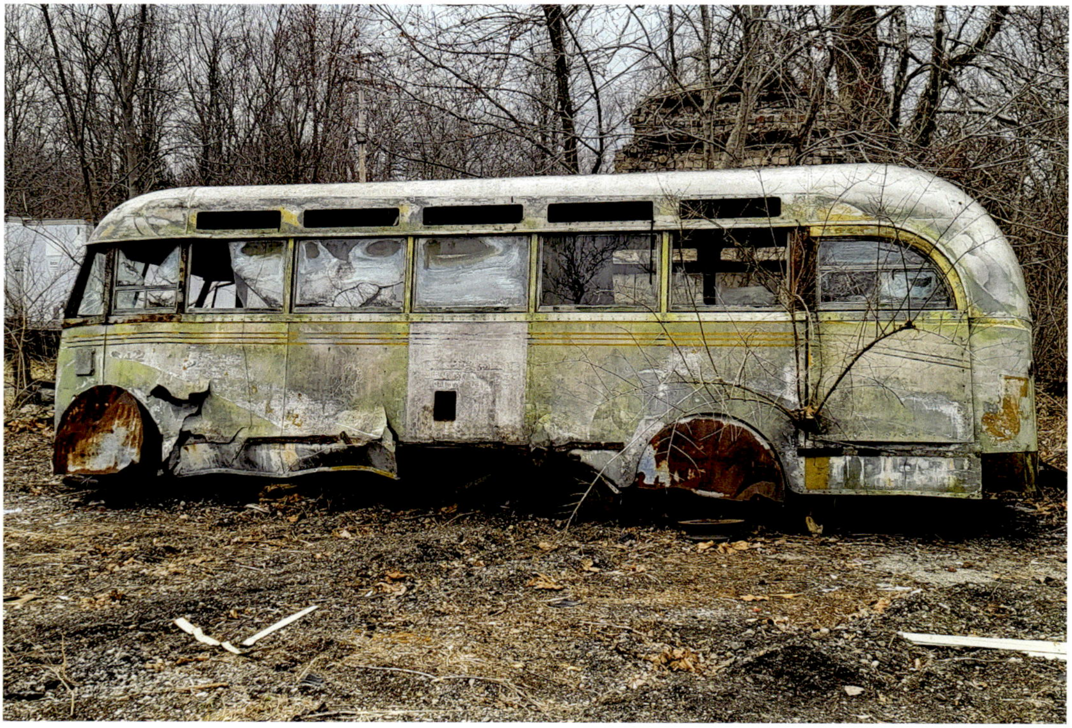

What looks to be a Mercedes-Benz O-3500.

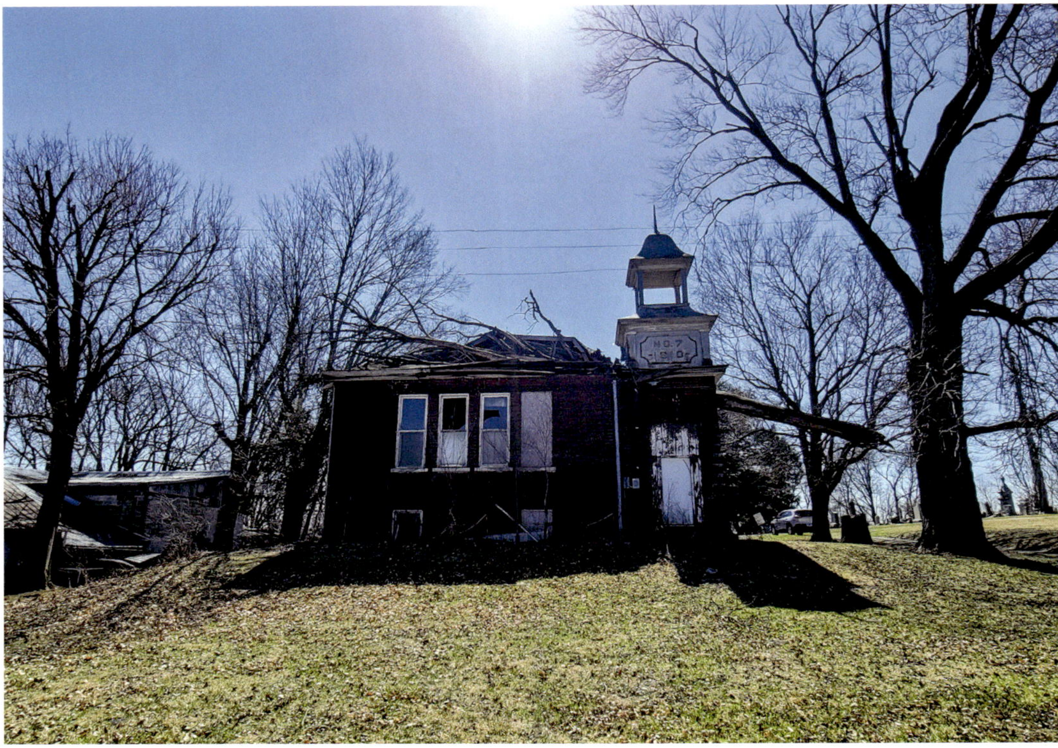

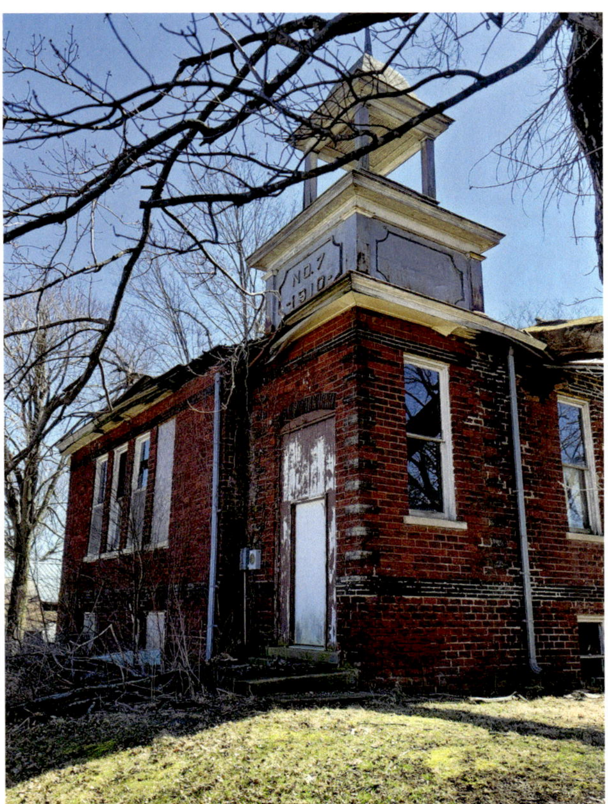

Above: School 7, built in 1910, was a fantastic side-of-the-road find on our way to a different location.

Left: Side view of the school showing the debris left over from the last storm.

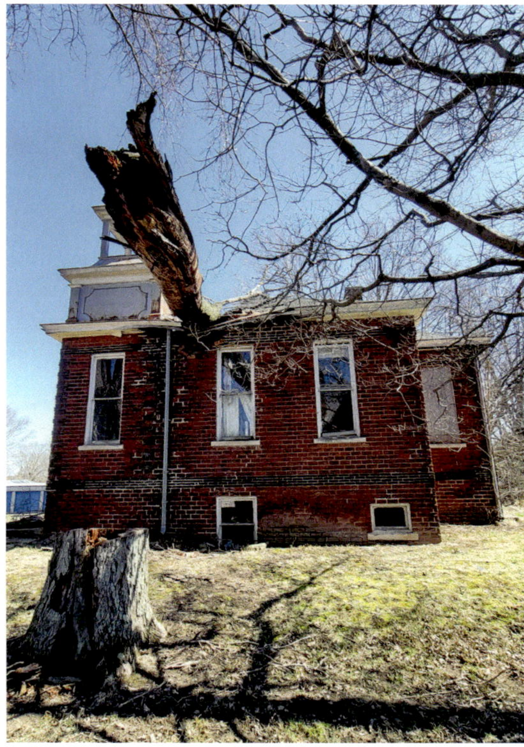

Right: The debris also included this entire tree that had collapsed onto the roof.

Below: Due to the lack of stable flooring, we had to get creative to get shots of the inside. This was taken through a basement window.

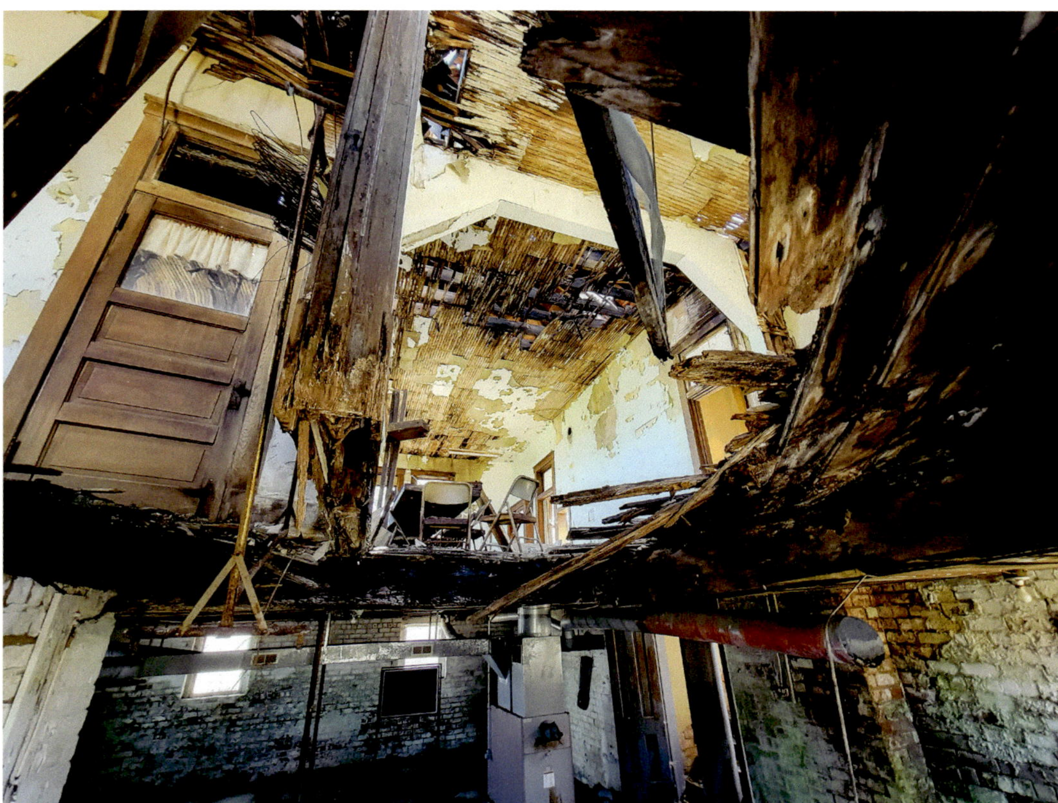

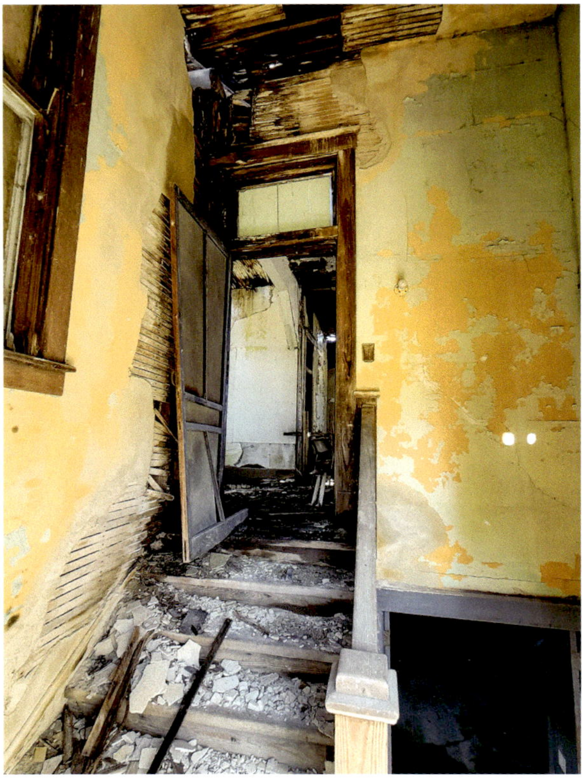

The back doorway to enter the school. It was pleasantly surprising to not see graffiti everywhere.

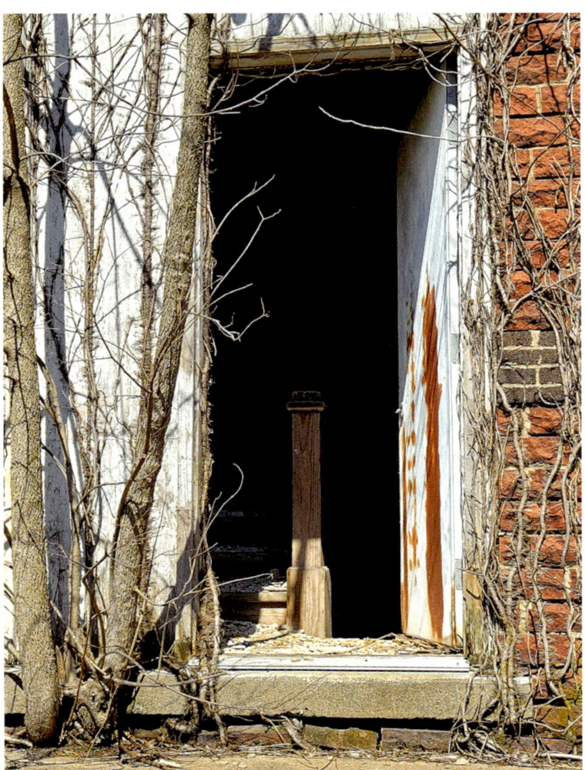

The back doorway before entering.

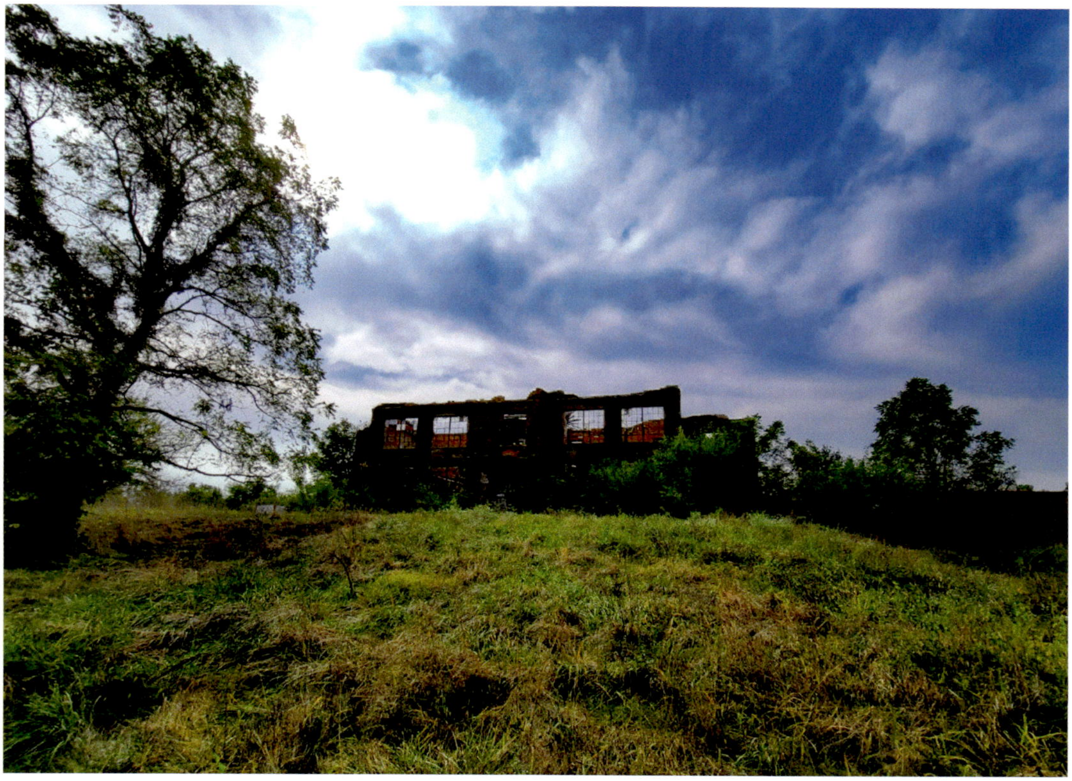

Above: On one of our road trips, we saw a sign for Jonestown, where we found the remains of this high school.

Right: Closer shot of the former Jonestown High school.

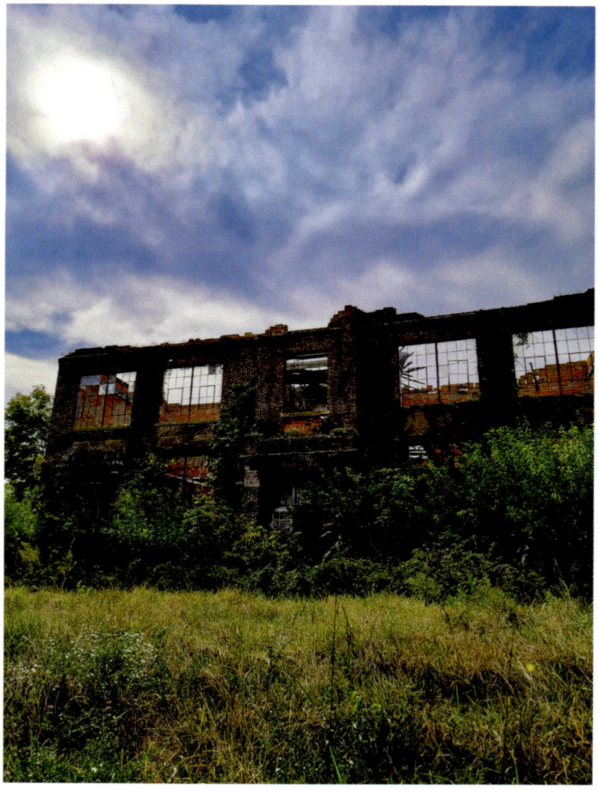

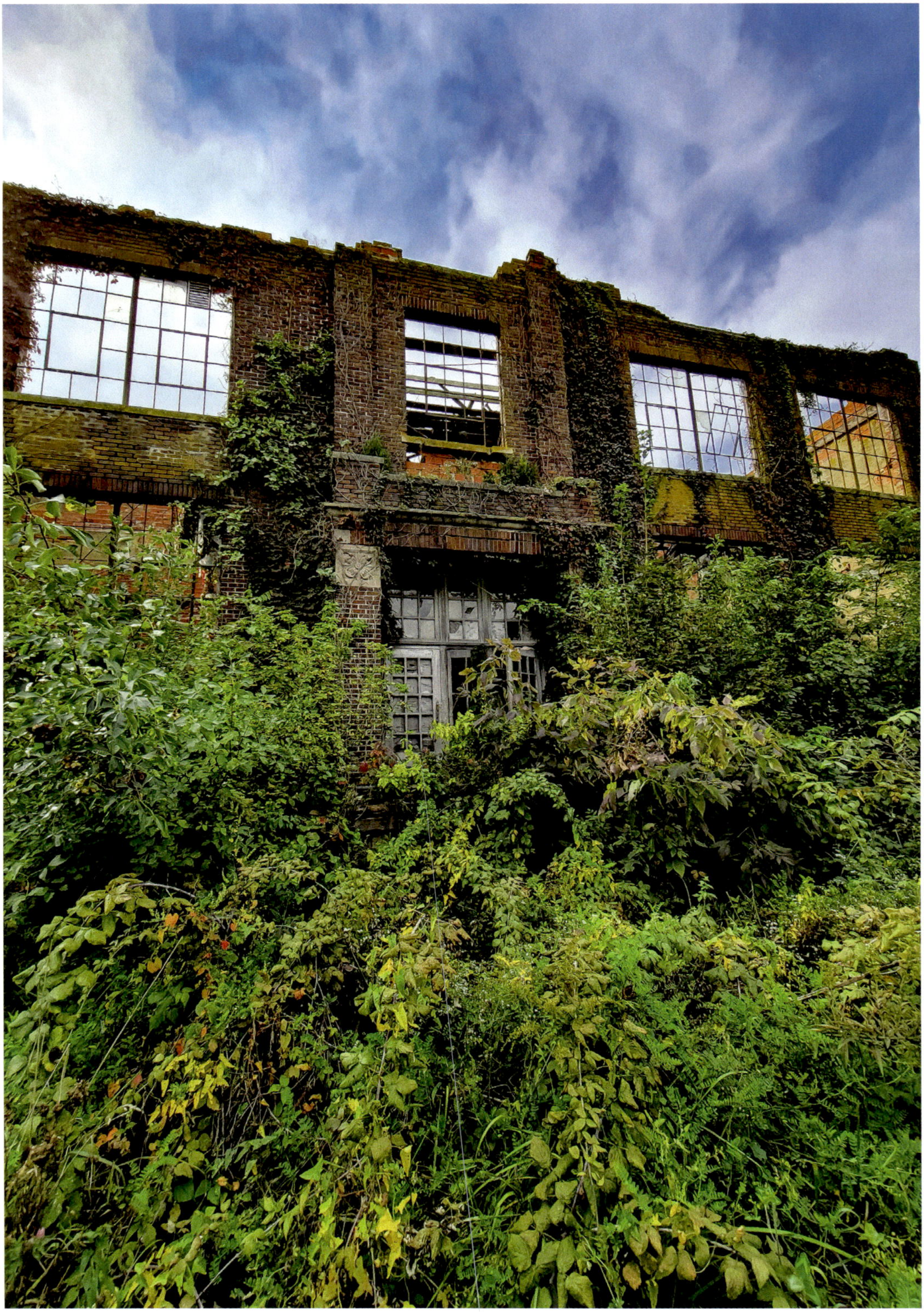

The school was completely overgrown and missing the entire roof.

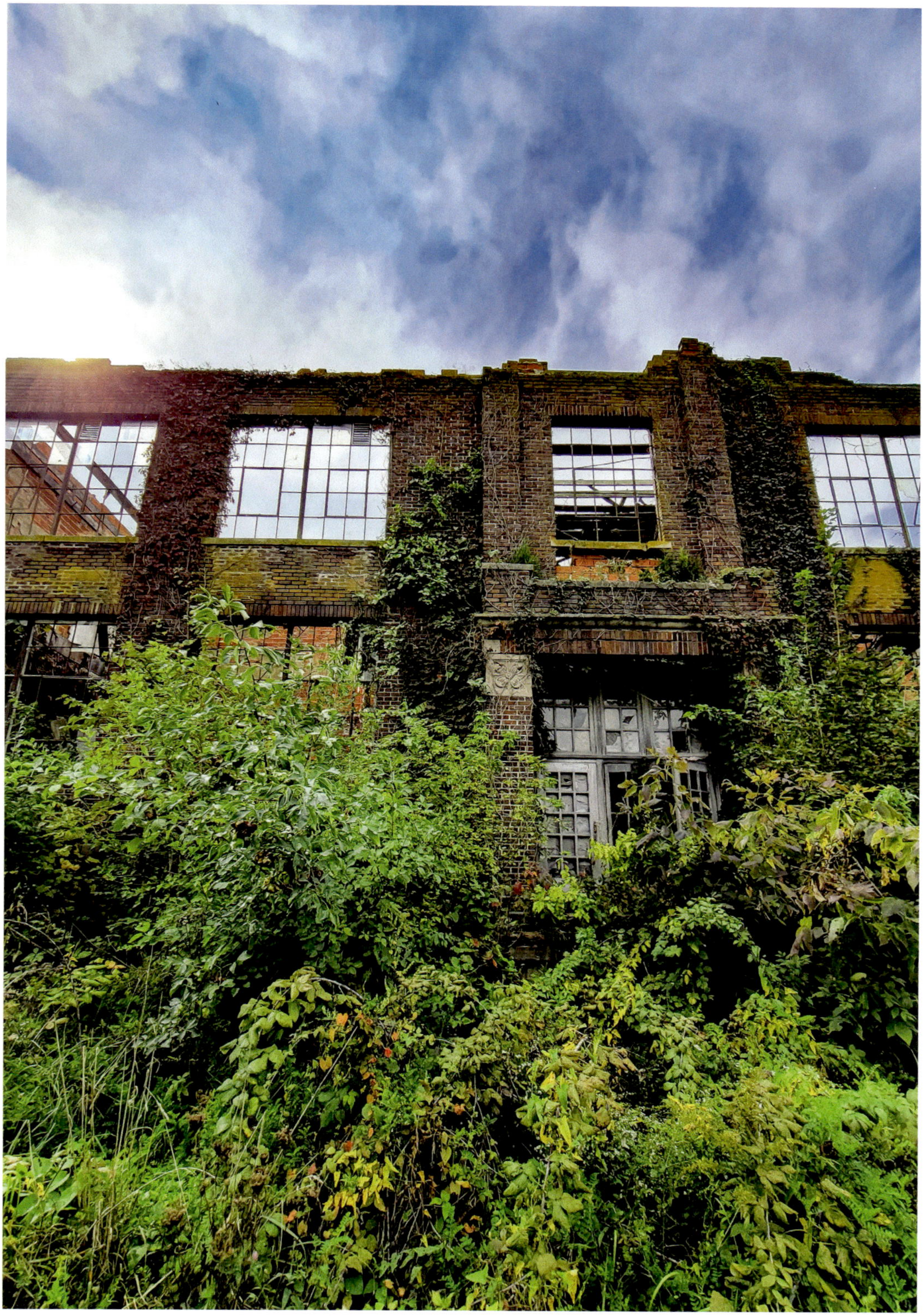

It was basically impossible to reach the front door without the use of lawn equipment, but there was still glass surrounding it.

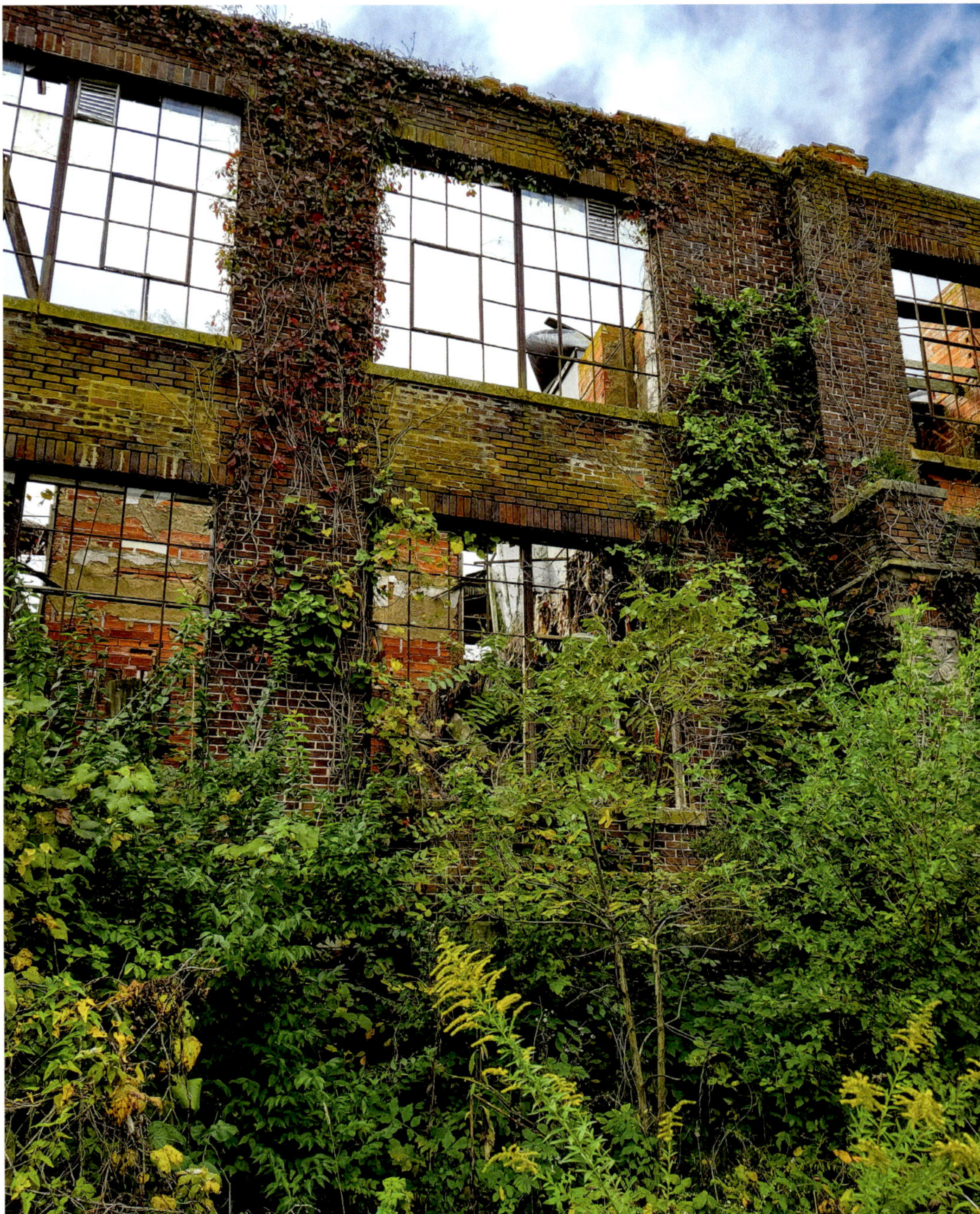

I like how some of the windows had been left open at some point and rusted in place.

REFERENCES

Boyce, Brian. "Work-Related Dispute Believed to Have Sparked Fatal Shooting." *Terre Haute Tribune-Star*, 10 Aug. 2009, tribstar.com/news/local_news/work-related-dispute-believed-to-have-sparked-fatal-shooting/article_4d55bcba-db3c-50ca-91e9-dcc7c388b12d.html.

Fashek, Allison. "M'ville Mom Shocked by Daughter's Death." *The North West Times*, 9 Mar. 2005, nwitimes.com/news/local/mville-mom-shocked-by-daughters-death/article_2193ee84-0bbe-54e7-a1ef-424f9ab88f9a.html.

Followell, Laura. *Rockville Health Care Facility Targeted for Probation.* 1 Feb. 2007, www.tribstar.com/news/local_news/rockville-health-care-facility-targeted-for-probation/article_0968e0af-73b2-5168-bf7b-bafd48d36d54.html.

Fujawa, Ed. "A Source of Controversy and Relief: The Marion County Poor Farm." *Class 900 Indy*, 19 May 2021, class900indy.com/post/a-source-of-controversy-and-relief-the-marion-county-poor-farm.

Hammer, Joanne. "Man Who Left Facility Likely Died of Seizure." *Terre Haute Tribune-Star*, 15 Feb. 2006, tribstar.com/news/local_news/man-who-left-facility-likely-died-of-seizure/article_4687f1fe-0ec0-5eca-a859-5596a532cf60.html.

Historian, Parke County. *Parke County Historian.* 26 Mar. 2013, facebook.com/page/206650956104945/search/?q=poor%20asylum.

Mitchell, Dawn. "Abandoned Thunder Island Water Park in Westfield Consumed by Nature and Graffiti." *The Indianapolis Star*, 25 Apr. 2019, indystar.com/story/news/history/retroindy/2019/04/25/abandoned-thunder-island-water-park-consumed-nature-and-graffiti-indianapolis-history/3549236002/.

Mullins, Nicole. "Health Department Survey Alleges Abuse at Rockville Nursing Home." *Terre Haute Tribune-Star*, 5 Oct. 2004, tribstar.com/

news/health-department-survey-alleges-abuse-at-rockville-nursing-home/article_2fa35fbe-9ead-583b-8ad9-f579148cf73a.html.

Partnership Parke County. *Partnership Parke County Newsletter*. January 2019, static1.squarespace.com/static/5ffc903204cb9a047fec2d32/t/600717bd86d9b062504be450/1611077565332/January+2019.pdf.

Protection and Advocacy for Individuals with Mental Illness. *2009 Annual Report*. The National Disability Rights Network , July 2010, ndrn.org/images/Documents/Resources/Publications/Reports/PAIMI-report_-2009.pdf.

Reavis, William C., and Lewis H. Mahoney. “Chapter V: The Administration of Special Educational Services: B. Special and Vocational Schools.” *Review of Educational Research*, vol. 10, no. 4, Oct. 1940, pp. 352–55.

SECURITIES AND EXCHANGE COMMISSION, Plaintiff-Appellee, v. Michael A. MAIO and Patricia C. Ladavac, Defendants-Appellants. Nos. 94-1233, 94-1234, 21 Mar. 1995, caselaw.findlaw.com/us-7th-circuit/1051303.html.

Tribune-Star Staff. “Former Lee Alan Bryant Employee Pleads Guilty to Battery.” *Terre Haute Tribune-Star*, 12 May 2004, tribstar.com/news/former-lee-alan-bryant-employee-pleads-guilty-to-bettery/article_1221963f-0504-5da7-bf4e-5ad99b3712b4.html.

Tribune-Star Staff. “Lee Alan Bryant Resident Dies after Walking Away from Nursing Home.” *Terre Haute Tribune-Star*, 25 Oct. 2006, tribstar.com/news/local_news/lee-alan-bryant-resident-dies-after-walking-away-from-nursing-home/article_4d3618da-9e50-599e-bc2f-a77a753c0cf0.html.

Trigg, Lisa. “Lee Alan Bryant Loses FSSA Funding Assistance Program.” *The Tribune-Star*, 19 July 2011, tribstar.com/news/local_news/lee-alan-bryant-loses-fssa-funding-assistance-program/article_c8ca1891-903e-50be-973d-d7efc42217b8.html